LIFE ON PLANET WWF

LIFE ON PLANET WWF

From Archbishops to Belly Dancers – My Time at WWF

C.Y. CHONG

Matador
9 Priory Business Park,
Wistow Road, Kibworth Beauchamp,
Leicestershire. LE8 0RX
Tel: (+44) 116 279 2299
Email: books@troubador.co.uk
Web: www.troubador.co.uk/matador

ISBN 978 1783065 134 (paperback)
978 1783065 172 (hardback)

British Library Cataloguing in Publication Data.
A catalogue record for this book is available from the British Library.

Typeset by Troubador Publishing Ltd, Leicester, UK

Matador is an imprint of Troubador Publishing Ltd

For family and in memory of my mother

CONTENTS

Herein lies a collection of delightful, captivating and easily readable humorous anecdotes – the perfect antidote for business people enslaved to the daily commute, dull office cubicles and standard boardroom décor.

Author Chiew Y. Chong lays bare the colourful aspect of WWF's inner soul, viewed through his eyes as their financial director and having spent many years himself in both the corporate world and that of the NGO.

Travelling from north to south, and east to west, Chiew takes us on a global jaunt with personalities and lifestyles that make up the fascinating world of philanthropy and social entrepreneurship.

Always insightful, yet leaving much room for the reader's imagination, the author recites countless tales of wisdom, honesty and naiveté – some distance indeed from the sophisticated voice of corporate marketing and political spin. Yet strangely enough, reading one of the chapters, "Freshly Cut Sandwiches", one detects the root cause of Wall Street's immense and complex greed in the primitive "double-your-money borrowing scheme" of the simple African witch doctor.

Chiew's power of observation and vernacular writing style makes this book a very pleasant and entertaining read. Written from the heart, it is an anthology to the diversity of mankind. One could only wish to have been part of the wonderful *tour du monde* as it occurred: a fly-on-the wall so to speak, or a travel companion perhaps.

Bob Bishop
Founder and President, ICES Foundation
Former Chairman and CEO of Silicon Graphics, Inc., a publicly listed Silicon Valley based corporation.

This book is about my journey into the world of a non-profit organisation – in this case, WWF. It's based on my personal first-hand experience of working in a conservation organisation and I believe it will convey a sense of the reality and the emotions of working at an NGO (Non Governmental Organisation).

I was initially hired as a finance manager. Three months later, at WWF International, I was promoted to the position of Director of Finance – a job typically referred to as CFO, Chief Financial Officer, in corporations. Although I was for many years the CFO at WWF, this book, however, does not address technical financial matters. There are already many good books on this subject. Rather, it's about a finance manager's non-financial experiences at an international NGO.

This book is about interesting and committed people I have met during my time at WWF. It is also about events, at times unusual and strange, at times humorous, the kind, I hope, that makes good anecdotes for a book. I have enjoyed writing it and it is my sincere hope that you, in turn, will have pleasure reading it.

Chiew Y. Chong F.C.A.
Former Director of Finance, WWF International

Goodbye Corporations

1

Do Fire Me

'Did I hear you right? You want me to fire you?' said Werner Oppliger, my manager. Werner is Swiss German and like many Swiss Germans I have met, he is efficient and disciplined. He possesses a strong authoritarian voice.

'What did you have for lunch? Too much wine?' he said.

'Yes,' I said, but that was not in response to the wine question.

At that time I was employed by "DEC", Digital Equipment Corporation, a major US global company. It was a prosperous firm, that ranked then as the second largest computer manufacturer in the world, after IBM. The multinational had been enjoying years of phenomenal growth. From the proverbial small garage, DEC, as we used to fondly call the company, had expanded across the globe. Geneva was the seat of the corporation's European headquarters. Worldwide annual revenues of the multinational were considerable. European sales alone – during the early 1990s – exceeded six billion US dollars annually.

I was one of the senior finance managers located at the European headquarters where I had occupied various job positions. At one time I was the European Software Services Controller. At another time I was the European Marketing Finance Manager; whilst at other times I headed different units within European Finance, which had a total headcount in excess of a thousand professionals.

After many years of heady growth, annual turnover of the company eventually slowed. Previously, the company had enjoyed consistent double-digit income increases. However, over the years, as the computer industry matured, prices had begun to crash, leading to increasingly noticeable slower sales growth.

Accustomed to good times for far too long, the corporation had become large and unwieldy. The headcount had become bloated, surpassing a hundred thousand employees worldwide. To adapt to the changing times, DEC had already begun retrenching staff for some years. It was under these circumstances that I had my somewhat unusual conversation with my boss. My motivation was simple. Given that the 'ship' was slowly sinking, I decided I might as well quit. Better quit before it was too late – and collect a "handshake" payment on my way out.

'We've only been firing lower level personnel – assistants, secretaries,' I said.

'So? What have you in mind?' Werner asked.

'We should also fire some executives.'

'Why?'

'To show that when we tighten the ship, all levels share the pain.'

'And who are you thinking of?'

'Me.'

A year later, on a Friday afternoon, whilst I was sitting in my office in Geneva, I received an unexpected telephone call. It was from Werner.

'Listen, you remember our discussions. When you asked to be fired?' he said.

'Yes.'

'We're running out of lower level employees. Do you still want it?'

'Yes.'

'You sure?'

'Absolutely not – but give it to me.'

My departure was thus confirmed, but had I made the right choice? At that moment I didn't know. What I did know was that my fate was sealed. I was to leave the comfortable and well-paid world of Fortune 500 multinationals.

At Home

I found myself at home. It felt good to be free – it was a period of excitement and anticipation. Liberated from the necessity to work for a living, well, at least for a while, I felt relaxed. For the foreseeable short-term, I no longer needed to worry about work and all its related stress. It was enjoyable to be at home, in a quiet residential area, a twenty-minute drive from Geneva's town centre. It was summertime. There was the garden, full of flowers. There was the pool – and there was my favourite long chair under the shade of the poolside umbrella.

The days passed by pleasantly. I would wake up late each morning. I would listen to the birds sing and read the newspapers. And each day, after a good lunch, I would take a nap. I had no complaints. Life was 'cool'.

However, when the third week began, I felt something was missing. Things did not seem right. My days had become long. They blended monotonously – one day merged into the next. Each day was like the one before – dull, with no special attraction. There was no "colour". When I met friends for dinner or drinks during the weekends, they buzzed with excitement, glad that the weekend had arrived. But I could not relate to those feelings. Too much free time was not good for me – I absolutely had to find something to do.

Join A New Industry?

I started to look for a job. I replied to various advertisements, including some posted in the FT – the *Financial Times*. One of the FT advertisements was by a London-based recruitment firm. A few weeks later, I found myself on their final shortlist. The job was based in the Far East – as regional general manager for a major music recording company.

The client, EMI, was a British multinational engaged in the music recording and publishing industry. They had multiple offices in Asia and wanted to hire a regional manager to consolidate their different businesses. I had experience working for global corporations and I hail from South-East Asia. The headhunters particularly liked it when I said I would be just as at home lunching with businessmen in a five star hotel as I would with other clients at roadside open-air food stalls. My discussions with the recruitment firm continued to progress well and soon reached an advanced stage.

'And where would be the location?' I had asked.

'It'll be entirely up to you. As the new regional manager – you'll have a free hand.'

'An Asian regional office should either be in Hong Kong or in Singapore. I recommend Singapore. I'm more familiar with Singaporean local customs,' I said.

'Sure, you'll make the final choice,' confirmed the British headhunters.

A meeting was arranged for me to meet with EMI.

But then, at this point, I changed my mind. For family-related reasons, I had decided I would not move to the Far East. I contacted the agency. I told them of my decision. I offered my apologies. They were not particularly pleased.

'I'm glad. I'd rather we continue living in Switzerland,' said Françoise, my Swiss wife. She had convinced me to settle in Switzerland in the first place.

'OK, we stay,' I replied.

PART TWO

7

Landing On Planet WWF

4

Passing Jaguar

It was a beautiful and sunny summer day. I was driving with my car's sunroof open. I admired the blue waters of Lake Geneva and the multiple rows of grape vines in the vineyards along the hillside. Not in any particular hurry, I drove my dark blue petrol-guzzling Jaguar saloon along the countryside. I listened to the catchy pop song belting out from my car's CD player. Then, as I negotiated a roundabout, I saw it. It stood there as though it had always done so. And ugly it was, the dull-grey, three-storeyed, rectangular-shaped office building. The unattractive structure aside, something else immediately caught my eye.

In front of the building, I saw two flags flying at full mast. They were on poles that stood in the garden. One was square-shaped and had a distinctive white cross against a red background – the Swiss flag. But it was the other flag that intrigued me – it was of a standard rectangular shape and, like the Swiss flag, it had only two colours, black and white this time. Its white background contrasted sharply with the large black Panda that occupied most of the space within the flag – it was smack right in the middle.

I pulled my car to the side of the road. Out came a notepad. I scribbled three letters and followed that with a question mark- 'WWF?'

I slipped the note into my shirt pocket and thought no more of the matter.

Why Not?

Later that day, in my study at my home, I was emptying my shirt pocket when I came across the note earlier scribbled. I hesitated for a second. Up to that point I had forgotten all about the strange Panda flag but now something was niggling me. I stared at the letters I had scribbled.

'I think I'll approach them: WWF,' I said to my wife.

'But will you like it? You've never worked for a non-profit organisation.'

'I know – I've always worked for corporations.'

A universe of financial statements, profits and other related matters.

'I think I'll write to them anyway. And see if anything happens,' I said.

I wrote to the Worldwide Fund for Nature. I mentioned I had left my last employers and should there be any interesting job openings, I could be interested. Within a few days, my telephone rang.

'Mr Chong?' said the caller.

'Yes?'

'My name's Solange. I'm calling from WWF human resources department. We've sent you a letter.'

'OK,' I said.

'But please ignore its contents,' she said.

'I don't get it,' I said.

'The letter's addressed to you – but not its contents. The envelope we sent to you was mixed up with another mail we sent out.'

'Oh.'

'Someone made a mistake. It was a case of the right letter placed in the wrong envelope. Or the wrong letter inserted in the right envelope. But anyway it's OK now. Since I now have you on the phone – let's fix a date for you to come meet us,' she said.

Job Interview

Two weeks later, the scheduled meeting date arrived.

'I'm off for the interview. I think I'll take your car,' I said to Françoise.

I put on a clean, crisp white shirt and grabbed a dark jacket as well as my black attaché case. Françoise's car then was a small white Volkswagen convertible. The car even had white seats. It was not a masculine type of car.

'Better your car. Never know what reactions I'll get if I roll up in mine,' I said.

'Yes, you'd better do that,' she replied.

I drove the car onto the large outdoor WWF car park, first passing the two flags that had caught my attention just a few weeks before. It was a car park with no trees: a large open asphalted area. I scanned the various vehicles already there. Most of them looked inexpensive and dated. As I walked towards the main entrance of the office, I was particularly intrigued by one vehicle. Parked near the entrance, it was an early model electric car. Mostly white with flecks of blue, it resembled a giant matchbox stood on its side. Fitted with four small tyres, large transparent plastic flaps for windows and two tiny upright seats, it looked terribly uncomfortable.

I entered the building and announced myself to the receptionist. After a short wait, a secretary met me. She led me up two flights of stairs. We entered a large room where there was a pile of cardboard boxes piled two metres high. The boxes served as a screen. Behind them sat the interview committee, which included Franck Schmidt, the then Director of Finance and Administration. Tim Geer, who subsequently became part of my team, was there too.

The interview proceeded smoothly.

'We're glad you could come,' said Franck.

'But you're too experienced – and too expensive,' said Tim.

'And you can well imagine – stock options are not customary here,' said Franck.

The whole discussion lasted no more than one hour.

I left, concluding that the meeting had no concrete outcome.

Reconnect

No news from WWF for a week.

Then, one afternoon, whilst I was at home watching Wimbledon live tennis, the telephone rang.

'Mr Chong?' said the caller.

'Yes, speaking,' I said.

It was WWF. I was asked if I could visit them again. They might now have something interesting to offer me.

A couple of days later, I returned to the WWF offices. I parked my car and re-entered the ugly grey building. A representative from the human resources department met me. She escorted me to a small meeting room – it was a cubicle with see-through glass walls.

'You're still too experienced and too expensive,' she said.

I listened attentively but did not reply.

'But we now have something closer to your profile. You might be interested. You could be our Finance Director.'

I liked the job – but not the salary. It was half my last pay cheque – and there were no stock options.

But life is such that we often have choices – and it is then up to each one of us to make decisions.

I made mine.

'I would be most interested,' I replied.

'Good. But before we can confirm your appointment, you'll have to meet "MEX".'

'"MEX"?'

'That's the Management Executive. It means the Director General and his two deputies. They make all the *real* decisions.'

And it was explained to me, with a mixture of reverence and some fear: MEX.

We scheduled a date for me to meet with the dreaded MEX.

Dreaded Trio

My day to meet up with the MEX members arrived. Firstly, I met with Charles de Haes, the Director General. Charles is Belgian. His English is impeccable – in terms of how he speaks and in his choice of words. Charles had previously been a senior marketing executive with Rothmans in South Africa. He had come to Switzerland to head WWF International at the request of the late Anton Rupert, founder of the Rembrandt Group of Companies.

When Charles arrived in Switzerland, he came with an ambitious goal – to raise ten million US dollars for WWF. This would be achieved via the "1001 Club". The late Prince Bernhard of the Netherlands was designated as the "One". And a thousand men and women would be invited to join him, hence the club name. The joining fee then was USD 10,000 per head. Starting from scratch, within three years, Charles had enlisted 1,000 names. His was an impressive feat. As there are 365 days in a year, his achievement within three years meant an average of one recruit every single day. Charles is a very able salesperson. But not only that, he also practises what he preaches.

'I tell them, in the nicest possible way, I myself have joined – have paid up. And since I'm poor compared to you, if I can pay, so can you – if you want to,' he once said to me.

My interview discussions with Charles proceeded smoothly. There were no hiccups.

Next, I met with Claude Martin, one of Charles' two deputies. Claude is Swiss. He had previously been the chief executive of WWF Switzerland and from there had moved on to WWF International. My meeting with Claude went well too.

Then came time to meet the third member of MEX, Henner Ehringhaus, the other deputy. Henner is German. However, he's someone who doesn't conform to the stereotypical German businessman, as we might imagine. When he talks, he is constantly smiling. At first I thought he was mocking me – then I realised he was just being friendly. Henner asked me many questions and his eyes glinted each time as he talked. He told me he used to be a senior executive with BASF, a leading German chemicals company.

As we came to the close of the interview, Henner, sitting behind his desk, leaned forward.

'I'm pleased you will be joining us,' he said.

'I'm pleased too,' I replied.

'When can you start?'

'I can come next week. But first – there are two "confessions" I need to make.'

'And what might these be?'

'I've an investment management company. It manages funds for some of my family and those of some friends. I intend to keep the company.'

'OK, that's not a problem – it's no competition to our activity.'

'Yes, I realise that – I just wanted to be open about it.'

'And the other issue?'

'I've a Jaguar car.'

'I know. I saw it. Not only it is big, your car, it's also one without a catalyser – but see you Monday…'

First Day

Early Monday morning, at home, whilst in the bathroom, I knotted a dark blue silk tie.

'How come you're putting on a tie?' asked Françoise. 'I thought you said the dress code there was casual,' she added.

'That's true,' I said.

'Then?'

'I want to send the right signals. That I'm serious and professional.'

'Which car are you taking?' she asked.

'Mine this time.'

The WWF office buildings are located adjacent to a large car parking area. All the offices situated on the car park side of the building have access to windows – openings with a commanding view of the entire parking area – and therefore of all comings and goings of vehicles (including the arrival of my Jaguar car).

I manoeuvred my car into an available slot at the car park. Leaving my car, I entered the building and walked to reach the top floor. I walked through an open door that led to a large communal room that housed a part of the finance team. As I entered, I saw a group of five people sitting behind their desks. They were young; probably in their thirties. Except for one woman, they were all men.

'Good morning,' I said.

Immediately, one of them, a man and the person nearest to me, stood up. Of medium height, Grumps – allow me to refer to him as Grumps – had black hair and an unfriendly look. He was dressed in a white long-sleeved shirt and in crumpled light-blue jeans. Turning his back to me, he made a loud announcement to his colleagues.

'What in the world are we coming to? Now we even hire finance managers who come to work driving polluting Jaguars.'

Taken aback by his outburst I was unable to immediately respond. However, a split second later, I recovered and I introduced myself.

I shook a few hands.

I did not shake Grumps'.

I asked if anyone knew where my office was.

'It's just here – it's the small office next to this one,' said Hanh Dinh, a female staff member, who orginates from Vietnam. Hanh is of medium height and, I later found out, a most kind and gentle person. She's someone who is always trying to be helpful.

She got up and showed me the door that led to my office.

When I approached the door, I saw that there was another door directly opposite – not far, about ten feet away. Between these two doors, to my left, was a wall. To my right was a small open area. This open area, a tiny cubicle – that was my office.

It was my second cultural shock of the morning. Firstly, I had to endure an unpleasant and uncalled-for rude public announcement by one of my staff members the very second I walked in. Then I was shown a small depressing cubicle that was to be my office. It was all rather peculiar, as new experiences go for me. Even the office furniture looked odd. These had been purchased second-hand and not a single piece matched. Each desk did not look like the other and the office chairs came in all shapes and sizes.

I put down my briefcase. I cleaned my desk.

'Where's the meeting room?' I asked Hanh. 'If you can please tell the finance team to meet me there,' I said.

We gathered at the conference room and took seats around the table. I sat on the end seat that had been left vacant for me. I mentioned how pleased I was to be at WWF. I asked the different staff members their names and what their job titles and functions were. I told them I would subsequently be meeting with each of them individually.

After the meeting, I returned to my office, the one with two doors. Although it was supposed to be my office, effectively it was a passageway. I first realised this when a tall man rushed into my office, entering through the first door and then, without even acknowledging my existence, immediately left through the other door. Then, two others came by, this time from the other side – and they just as quickly exited through the opposite door. And so it was, people constantly walking in and out of my work area. It was most distracting – quite impossible working conditions. And all this happened within the first hour of my settling into my new 'office'.

During this same time period, my "friend", Grumps, passed in and out of my office twice. And each time, when he had dashed into my office, he rushed out again through the other door – and always in a noisy way, as though he had to run to catch a departing train.

I decided I had to do something about the traffic.

I left my chair, went to the door and closed door "two". Then I locked it.

I returned to my desk.

No sooner had I sat down was when Grumps came barging in once again. He came in through door one. He headed for door two. He pumped the door handle violently.

'Who locked this door?' he demanded as he glared at me.

'I did,' I said.

Without a word, he stormed out, returning to where he had come from.

All this was, by then, too much for me.

I picked up my telephone and I called Henner, one of the two deputy director generals.

'Henner, I must see you,' I said.

'OK, come over.'

I made my way to the red building located nearby where Henner was.

I found myself in Henner's office. His was a pleasant and well-decorated office, quite unlike my cubicle. Henner welcomed me to WWF. He asked me how my first day at work was proceeding.

I narrated to him my early morning special welcome speech from Grumps – the unnecessary insolence and his uncalled-for aggressive attitude. I then explained to him the problem of the doors and how unpleasant he was when I told him I was the person who locked door 'two'.

'What do you propose?' Henner asked.

'This is my first day – but either he goes or this will be my last day,' I said.

Henner did not reply.

He picked up his telephone.

He called Charles, the Director General. He briefed Charles. Henner kept silent as he listened to Charles' comments.

'OK, I'll tell him that,' he said.

Henner put his phone down.

'So what did Charles say?' I said.

'To congratulate you – we should have fired him years ago…'

Second Day

On day two, I was sitting in my cubicle, reading the CVs of the various finance department staff members, when Hanh entered.

'The meeting's set for this afternoon at four,' she said.

'What meeting? I'm not aware of any meeting,' I said.

'The finance department staff – they would like a discussion with you.'

Four o'clock arrived. I re-entered the same conference room where I had been the morning of the day before.

I did not see a friendly look on anyone's face. All the finance team staff members had a tense look – the atmosphere was "heavy", to put it mildly.

As was the case the previous day, one seat had been left empty – that would be for me.

I had hardly sat down when one of the team members spoke. His tone was aggressive.

'I heard – our colleague, Grumps, was fired yesterday. Is that true?' he demanded.

'Yes – that's correct,' I said.

'We want to know why you did that without first asking us.'

'I can understand it – if some of you are upset. But please remember, I was hired to manage this finance department. That being the case, I will do whatever is necessary.'

Absolute silence followed.

I let the silence reign for a few seconds – then I said, 'If there are no other comments, then I have a subject I wish to bring up.'

There were no other comments.

'I need to have some statistics compiled. This will probably take two to three days. Who can do this for me?'

I looked around and waited. There were no volunteers. A few seconds later – which seemed much longer – Peter Dickinson, a British chartered accountant who had also recently joined WWF, spoke.

'I'll do it,' he said.

Relieved, I thanked him and I closed the meeting.

Third Day

When the third day came, I decided it was time for me to take inventory – to assess the financial management of the organisation. I took a blank piece of paper. On it I outlined three columns. For the first column, I put in as the header the word "Good". On column two I wrote "Average". And lastly, for column three, the header I put in was "Bad". For the rows, I prepared a comprehensive listing of the major financial criteria expected of a well-managed finance department.

Then I systematically ranked, one by one, the then financial management of WWF. When I looked at the results I saw I had rated "Good" only once; "Average" was rated twice and all else had been rated as "Bad". I looked out through the small window. It was dark outside and the rain was pouring down. It looked miserable. Sitting inside, I found it just as depressing as I reviewed my sheet of paper with the appalling scores. Almost everything in terms of financial matters (for example, budgeting and forecasting procedures) was, at that time, lacking. Appropriate professional systems and procedures were just not there. The financial management that was in place was more that suited a small charity, rather than what would be proper and professional for a large not-for-profit organisation.

Maybe I had made the wrong choice?

Perhaps I should not have come to this NGO?

What am I doing in such a place where all the financial systems needed so much improvement?

The ball was squarely in my court. It was all up to me – my choice. I could either throw it all up by quitting – or I could continue.

I hesitated – I mulled it over.

I decided to stay – to finish what I had started.

It would be quite a challenge. I decided to face it – I was determined not to back out.

And hopefully I would not later regret my decision…

PART THREE

23

Early Years

Cleaning Up Finances

During my first few years at WWF, I spent most of my time improving the financial management systems. Although the public is not always aware, finances for an NGO (Non Governmental Organisation) are in fact far more complex than those for a corporation.

Why is that so?

I can best explain through two examples.

Example Number One:

When donors grant funds, they often specify their requirements for the exact use of their money. This is particularly so when the sums donated are substantial. That being the case, it becomes absolutely necessary to track the flow of the funds, from receipt, right up to the spending of the monies. Such tracking is to ensure that funds are spent in full accordance with the wishes of the donor. In instances where the amount received is important, the spending would also have to be reported back, in detail, to the donor or donors.

Example Number Two:

Funders of WWF include governments and aid agencies. It is not unusual for such funders to send their own team of auditors for routine checks. When that happens, sometimes even up to three teams of auditors would be involved. Firstly, the external statutory auditors; then, there would be WWF's internal auditors and, finally, the auditors of the funding agency.

Getting WWF's finance management systems up to speed was hard work – technical finance work, but entirely necessary. I hired various professional staff and, gradually, all needed and appropriate financial management systems were installed. I wanted to first make sure that financial matters were up to speed at the International Secretariat, prior to moving on to address the finances of project offices in different countries.

One Sunday I was sitting at the bar of my tennis club in Geneva, having a drink with Gerard Weyer, a long-time friend and tennis partner.

'How's it going, your new job?' he said.

'It's quite a challenge. Almost everything needs to be improved. But step by slow painful step we're getting there. I've been hiring the right people.'

'Do you get to see field conservation work?'

'Up to now, no, not yet. Sometimes I wonder if I'll ever see any wildlife in this job. If it continues like this I'll get bored – I might even quit.'

But there was no need to have been impatient.

I was soon to be involved with field projects and wildlife – commencing with Gordon's lions.

Gordon's Lions

Gland, Switzerland

I was sitting in the main conference room at the WWF International Secretariat's offices. It was a large room with an amphitheatre arrangement, whereby rows and rows of seats were in a semi-circle, overlooking the floor area in the centre. With me was Gordon Shepherd. It was a very large room for two people to have a conversation – but since that was the only available place that morning, we used the room. Gordon was a colleague. He's from Scotland and at one time worked for Margaret Thatcher. Gordon's also different from most of the other colleagues – he always wears a kilt during official functions. But most importantly, he often has good ideas for a laugh. Looking for a different opening for a talk I was to give, I asked him if he had any suggestions – and he was responding to my request.

'Last night I was having dinner with my friend the bishop,' said Gordon.

'How come you know a bishop?' I asked.

Gordon did not reply to my question.

'My friend the bishop, he's from Rome. He came to visit me. As we were tucking into the dessert, he asked me, 'Have you heard the true story – of the Christians and the lions? In the Coliseum, there was a huge lion, a ferocious beast. Whilst Nero sat in the shade under an awning, the Roman soldiers untied the first Christian. At the other end of the arena, a caged lion roared. The soldiers raised the iron bars of the cage and the hungry lion came rushing out. It headed straight for the Christian. The Christian trembled. The lion roared and it quickly devoured the poor chap.

After the soldiers had cleared up the mess following that meal, they sent the next Christian into the arena. The bloodthirsty crowd cheered as the lion rushed up to the second Christian. The lion roared and ate the second man too.

Then came the third Christian's turn – an old man, small and frail. The lion rushed towards him – it roared. The lion opened its huge jaws. And exactly at that moment, the man raised his right hand. Holding his hand to one side of his mouth, he whispered in the lion's ear. With a terrified look in its eyes, the lion immediately rushed out.

Nero demanded that a second lion be sent in. A bigger and more ferocious beast was brought into the arena. This lion hurried to the Christian. It gave a noisy roar. The Christian raised one hand and he again whispered. The lion trembled. With its tail between its legs, it scrambled out.

Nero, now upset, yelled for a third lion. The third lion arrived. It walked in slowly, extremely slowly. It had a menacing look – and when it roared, all the walls of the Coliseum shook. There was a hush as the spectators held their breath. This would be it. Surely now, the poor fellow would be done for.

The old man approached the lion. He spoke softly. The crowd gasped. They stood up in shock when they saw the lion rushing out.

By now, Nero was frustrated. What was the empire coming to when small men can make fierce lions flee? But the Emperor had no choice – he had to set the Christian free.

Calling for the man, Nero said, "Christian, you deserve it. I set you free. But before you go – I have to ask you a question. Tell me, what do you whisper to the lions?"

"Sire, I told them – if you eat me, after the first course you'll have to make a speech…"

Financial Systems Established

It took time, during my initial years at WWF, to establish the necessary financial systems on the home front. Only after that had been accomplished was I able to change focus. I then shifted from addressing finances at the Secretariat to that of the field offices in the different countries in which WWF operates. I also began supporting colleagues in the fundraising department. My work thus became substantially more varied and interesting.

As the experiences and events I wish to recount occurred at different points in time – and sometimes simultaneously – I have grouped them under four different subject categories as follows:

- Environmental Conservation
- Royalty
- Fundraising
- Business Unusual

Environmental Conservation

Rebellious Youngsters

Bayanga, Central African Republic

As part of my responsibilities to review and advise on finances in the field, I visited a project office in the Central African Republic. This office was located in Bayanga, an area that has lush vegetation. To get there I had to travel in a single-propeller plane, which landed on a tiny dirt airstrip.

Whilst there, one afternoon, after lunch, I was walking back to the office together with a German WWF colleague when he spoke to me.

'You know, I'm an ant specialist,' he said.

Many a time I have observed ants whilst visiting natural history museums. Through the glass walls of their enclosures I have seen them scurrying through tunnels, carrying food, constantly on the move. Some ants, the leaf-cutter ants, even practise "farming". These ants cultivate fungi, regularly feeding the fungi with freshly cut plant material. Not only that, they even know how to keep their cultivation free from pests and moulds.

'That's unusual. I've never met an ant specialist. What do we call someone who studies ants?' I asked.

'A mymecologist.'

'Ants seem well organised,' I said.

'If you observe them, you'll be amazed to see how well their society is structured,' he said.

As we neared the project office, my colleague stopped.

'This you must see. Look closely at the ground.'

'I see plenty of ants,' I said, observing a long troop of trailing ants on the dry gravel track.

'With a bit of luck – I'll be able to show you something interesting. Come – squat down over here,' he said.

We squatted down to better view the ants.

The ants were small and red. They were rushing about frantically. Each ant was in a hurry. From my childhood days in Asia, I knew these ants were not to be underestimated. Being small and red, they were like red spicy chillies. The smaller and redder they are – the more powerful the kick. And their redness was probably Nature's way to warn onlookers to keep away.

'Look carefully,' he said.

I looked.

'Ants often have two-way traffic. Those going one way would touch and thus "greet" ants coming from the other way. After each "hello" they would continue on their respective ways. But look at this lot. Notice how they're all heading in the same direction.'

'How come?' I asked.

'Means they're going home. Either that or they have decided there was nothing to eat where they were. Or they had finished a meal.'

'Amazing – ants going home,' I said.

'Follow me,' my ant expert said, as he stood up.

We followed the ant trail in the direction from whence they had come. A few paces further on, my guide stopped. He did not say a word. He just stood still, observing the ants.

'I thought so,' he said.

'What?' I asked.

'In our society we have those who follow rules. There are also those who encourage others to follow.'

'And the relevance?' I asked.

'Sometimes juveniles may need some persuasion,' he said.

'So?'

'Look down here. You see these ants? They're of the same size. These are adults. See how they all move. With purpose and in the same direction.'

I looked. He was right.

'Now observe the ones over here.'

He pointed his index finger towards the end of the line. I bent down. I saw more ants. These ones were smaller. They were not moving in the same direction. They were moving about randomly, without much purpose.

'These are the juveniles. Much less disciplined, this lot. Now wait.'

I waited.

'Here they come,' he said

'Who's coming?' I asked.

He pointed to some larger adult ants that had just arrived at the scene. They approached the youngsters. I saw the adults nudge the younger ants. And each time, the juvenile so pushed instantly perked up – and followed in the direction of the line of trailing ants. The wonders of Nature…

Freshly Cut Sandwiches

Libreville, Gabon

A standard routine in all field offices is that cash is regularly withdrawn from banks. There are always expense items that need to be settled with cash payments. To procure the required cash, an office employee would be sent to the bank and small amounts of cash would be obtained. Such activity would typically be delegated to a relatively junior staff member.

One day, to the surprise of his colleagues, the WWF country representative in Gabon decided he would himself go to the bank. Having thus volunteered himself, he systematically approached each project executant (person responsible for the management of field projects). He enquired about their cash needs and ended each visit collecting cheques to be cashed on the project executants' behalf.

Having done the rounds and collected a bundle of cheques, the representative went to the bank. Whilst there, he withdrew a large amount of cash – but not a single dollar of this cash arrived at the WWF offices.

Interviewed by his manager, the man said, 'Obtaining the cash from the bank, I decided to go home. I wanted to say hello to my wife. Then whilst at home, I received a phone call. It was from a government minister. He requested an instant meeting and I agreed.'

'At this point – you still had the cash with you?' his manager, Laurent Somé, asked.

'Yes, I had the cash. I went to see the minister. We had good discussions. After our meeting, I made my way back to the office. En route I felt hungry so I decided to get something to eat. Arriving at the bakery, I parked my car alongside the road and I entered the shop.'

'Then what happened?'

'I bought cakes and I returned to the car. Once inside the car, I checked if the money was still there but it was gone.'

'Where in the car did you leave the cash?'

'In the glove compartment.'

'Did you lock the car?'

'No.'

In response to the various highly improbable explanations, WWF called the police and the man was arrested. That would have been the end of this peculiar tale. But no, this was not the case.

I was asked to help sort out the problem, whereupon I boarded a plane and arrived in Libreville. The next day, Laurent (Laurent, from Burkina Faso, was the manager in charge of a few West African countries, including Gabon) and I consulted with a law firm in Libreville. The lawyer who met us was someone bright, educated and highly articulate. He certainly made an excellent impression on me and he seemed to know his job.

'I think it's a case of the witch doctors,' he said.

'Come again – you're not serious?' I said.

'I am – it's a double-your-money scheme. I'm sure that's what happened. Even though he stole the cash, your man only meant to "borrow" it – if only for a day or two. To give to his witch doctor.'

'And why would he do that?' I asked.

'Some of our witch doctors are dishonest. They have this "get rich quick" scam whereby they ask for bank notes and promise to return a stack double in thickness the next day.'

'No – just like in Hollywood movies?' I said.

'You'll have to believe me. In my country, a part of the population – at times even educated people – has great faith in witch doctors. They believe the witch doctors can double their money. Of course what really happens is that a bigger stack would be returned. There would be real bank notes – but only at each end, sandwiching freshly cut newspaper in between…'

Wicker Chair Lady

Bayanga, Central African Republic

I went to visit an African field project in the Dzanga Sangha region. This region forms part of the Congo Basin forest – the world's second largest forest. WWF has a project in this region. It's called "the Dzanga Sangha project" – often referred to as "TNS", this being the initials for the "Tri-National of the Sangha".

Why such a name? Why Tri-National? It's because the project covers the boundaries of three nations. It encompasses the national parks of the Central African Republic, the Democratic Republic of Congo and Cameroon.

I boarded a small single-propeller aircraft. The plane touched down at Bayanga in the Central African Republic and I was driven to a place called Doli Lodge. Of African style and located by a river, the lodge has accommodation which consists of timber huts erected high on long stilts. At the side of each hut I saw wooden steps.

Climbing the steps, at the top I reached an open veranda; from there was access to a main door that led directly to the bedroom. The room had an adjoining bathroom and a decent clean bed. There was crisp white bed linen, complete with the ever-present white mosquito netting hanging over the bed.

Staying in the hut I had the impression I was much immersed in nature – granted, it was nature *with* comfort; not the same as staying in a makeshift tent in the forest. However, I felt isolated as the location was remotely situated – far away from the normal hustle and bustle of city life. Each hut was relatively well separated from the next and nearby were countless tall trees and thick bushes. I heard monkeys shrieking, I looked in the direction of the sound. There were a number of small-sized adult monkeys amongst the trees. Observing them, I made a mental note to not forget to properly lock the hut's door.

As dusk arrived, I met WWF field colleagues for dinner. We gathered in the "dining room" – an open-air raised platform built on stilts. The platform consisted of wooden planks placed one alongside the other, with a small gap between each – this meant there was not much need to do any sweeping since dirt and dust would fall through, between the "cracks". When we had finished the meal, a colleague from Germany proceeded to prepare coffee. He had brought with him an elaborate personal coffee-making machine.

'I always travel with these,' he said as he proudly displayed his matching coffee cups.

'We're lucky to be able to enjoy freshly made coffee and drink from proper cups, whilst being miles from any town,' he said.

'What more can anyone ask for?' I said.

As I drank my coffee, I admired the panoramic view. There was the wide meandering river, flowing ever so slowly through an endless stretch of lush greenery by its banks. Enjoying the view, I remembered my lunch chat with a friend the previous week. In Geneva, we had discussed the deadly Ebola virus – it had been on the news lately.

'In Europe, Ebola's in the news again. I heard it on TV – Ebola outbreaks in Africa. Apparently it's also here, in this region,' I said.

'That's true,' an African colleague said.

'Where's Ebola happening – I mean relative to where we are?' I said.

'Don't worry. It's quite far away,' he said.

'Quite far would mean how far?' I said.

'Downstream – two hours by boat…'

I gulped my hot coffee and decided it was time to change the subject.

Early next morning we set off to visit a large open clearing within the forest where the elephants were known to assemble – and where elephants gather, so do humans. The elephants are there for the minerals beneath the soil and the humans for the elephants.

'You know, on any given day there would be at least forty – and sometimes even as many as one hundred elephants at the *Bai*,' said my guide.

Bai means a clearing in the forest.

'Wow, that must be quite a sight,' I said.

'It is. Keen elephant observers even call the place "Elephant Heaven".'

'The elephant observers – what do they actually do?' I asked.

'They watch the elephants. They observe them closely and they take extensive notes.'

'Are there other animals?'

'Yes – forest buffalos, hogs and bongos.'

'What are bongos?'

'They are an antelope species with white stripes. And they are unusual because both males and females have horns.'

To get to the *Bai*, we had to first travel by jeep. Driving for an hour and a half, we went along some extremely narrow gravel paths. The "roads" were all uneven. The jeep rocked up and down and tree branches constantly scraped along the sides of the vehicle. We came across a horizon white pole: a barrier that blocked the road. My guide got off the jeep, approached the barrier and lifted it. We continued our bumpy journey driving through the thick forest.

We arrived at a small open area where there was barely space to park the jeep. Leaving the vehicle, we walked towards the banks of a stream.

'Now you'll get your feet wet,' said my guide.

I removed my shoes and, holding shoes in hand, I followed him into the water as we waded downstream. I felt uncomfortable. As soft mud squished between my toes, I could at the same time feel the cool water coming from behind me flowing evenly around my calves. What if I stepped on something – something unfriendly that bites?

After our knee-deep wade, we left the stream. We trekked up a hill following a steep forest path. I felt relaxed. This was until I came across a small wooden plank nailed to a narrow tree trunk. Inscribed on the board were the following words:

"In case of elephant attack, do not run.
Stand behind a tree and keep still."

Good advice but how would it be possible to stay cool if attacked? Elephants are large animals – not to mention the nerve-wracking cries they would emit to further terrify any poor soul so menaced.

We continued our walk. An hour later we arrived at the *Bai*. It was as large as thirty football fields combined. With its saltpans and its waterholes, it attracted a huge variety of animals and birds. I had never seen so many elephants gathered in one single place. Some were arriving and others were going but the majority were almost standing still. The "almost standing still" ones were all busy, but in the laboriously slow-moving elephant kind of way. They probably only move fast when angered.

We approached a raised wooden observation platform area built on stilts. All of a sudden, my guide stopped talking in his usual voice. He was almost inaudible.

'I'm whispering because we mustn't disturb the elephants,' he said.

We ascended the steps to reach the platform. I took possession of an armchair. I noticed a woman was already there, seated in a corner of the observation deck. She paid no attention to us and she looked most preoccupied with her binoculars and her notebook.

'Please keep silent,' my whispering guide decided to remind me.

I kept quiet as told. We observed the elephants. Although the platform had a roof, it was nevertheless still uncomfortably hot and extremely humid. It was also quiet, as I did as I was told (remained silent). My guide, on the other hand, did not.

He whispered to me again.

'She's American. She's been coming here every day – for years. She recognises all of them and has given names to each elephant,' he said.

The sight of so many elephants gathered in one single place was hypnotizing. However, an hour later, merely watching slow-moving elephants, with no talking permitted, sitting in a comfortable chair, whilst in the tropics, I almost dozed off.

I saw elephants in slow-motion "action". There were elephants walking, elephants drinking, elephants standing still, elephants gently waving their trunks up and down. Apart from that, nothing much happened. Eventually, some of the elephants plodded away. They left the clearing as they slowly trundled back to the forest.

To my relief, my guide finally said it was time to leave. As we descended the steps of the platform, I saw the American lady was still there. She maintained full concentration, watching the few remaining elephants, whilst sitting on her corner wicker chair…

Game Wardens Shoot Poachers

Bayanga, Central African Republic

In Bayanga, we were driving along a gravel road on the way to a WWF project office. The road we were on cut right through the forest. As the jeep bumped up and down, I saw uniformed game wardens walking single file along the narrow road. Dressed in safari-style outfits, they had rifles slung over their shoulders.

'The wardens – they carry real guns?' I asked the driver.

'Yes, of course.'

'They use them if they come across poachers?'

My travelling companion grinned.

'Yes, they do fire those rifles,' he said.

'What happens then? The poachers get wounded and some die?'

'No, no, nothing like that – the wardens, they shoot in the air,' he said.

'The poachers - they might as well continue poaching,' I said.

'They too fire shots in the air. Then, when both groups are done with the shooting, everyone goes home.'

As we continued our journey, the driver explained the seemingly strange gunfight to me. It so happened that in that particular region, the wardens and the poachers knew each other well. Either they were from the same village or from villages nearby. The poachers would in fact be accosted and charged when they returned home. It was most unusual but certainly practical: this African version of *High Noon at OK Corral*.

19

Locked Safe

Youkadouma, Cameroon

'What happened?' I asked, as I entered my colleague's office at WWF Secretariat in Switzerland. I'd been told robbers had attacked the Youkadouma project office.

'Do you know the details?'

'The raiders came one night, three of them. Apparently they tied up the guard. Then they tried to open the safe – but couldn't, so they left.'

'So there was no burglary?'

'No, not that night – but they returned the next evening. This time they came with reinforcements and they carted off the entire safe…'

Million Dollar Smile

Antananarivo, Madagascar

Sheila O'Connor, who now lives in Britain, was at one time the WWF Country Representative in Madagascar. She had invited me to visit to review project finances and to help advise her finance staff. So off I went. On day three, I was having morning coffee with some WWF conservation department staff members when one of them said:

'You have to go to the market. Today's a good day to do that – and you must especially see the traditional medicines. Jacques is an expert in this area; he'll show you around.'

I took the advice. I contacted and met with Jacques, a tall black African. He had a friendly face and he seemed constantly happy.

We boarded a white four-wheel drive and headed for the market. Jacques' job was to understand traditional cures – how they work and to record them.

We arrived at the market and we walked around. It was clear that Jacques was well known to many of the participants. We received warm spontaneous greetings from various sellers of market produce. I saw fresh vegetables offered for sale. I passed butchers selling meat. I saw chickens wandering around. I even saw a man sleeping on the floor, whilst a chicken pecked at his trouser pockets – a different kind of pickpocket.

We approached another market stall.

'This lady: she sells special leaves – they are a cure for headaches,' Jacques said.

We walked on further.

'This other person: she sells exotic plants – it's a cure for arthritis.'

Then we came across a wooden stand, behind which stood a tall woman. She gave us a broad smile. She had a dark complexion and perfect-looking white teeth. Because of the contrast with her dark complexion, her teeth looked even whiter.

'Meet Josephine – her leaves are excellent. They are used as toothpaste…'

Room Service

Nouakchott, Mauritania

'André tells me you'll be an asset if you join us,' said Sylvie Goyet to me.

Sylvie's half-French and half-Swiss. In the past she worked at WWF but had already left when she had her conversation with me. The André she was referring to was André Hoffmann, an important Swiss businessman. André is the son of Luc Hoffmann and like his father, someone much committed to the conservation cause.

'Will you do it? The assignment's pro bono – but then you'll be helping the environment,' added Sylvie.

She was speaking in her capacity as President of "BACOMAB", a Mauritanian Conservation Trust Fund. The invitation was for me to join the trust fund's board.

'I'll have to think about it,' I said.

A week later, I telephoned Sylvie. I told her I would be delighted to help.

She gave me the dates of the next board meeting to be held in Mauritania.

'As it will be your first trip there – I propose you visit the project site. It's only a few hours' drive from Nouakchott.'

'Good idea – but I have a question. What about the kidnapping risk?' I asked.

'Don't worry, we'll disguise you – have you wrapped in local clothing…' she replied.

The following month, I boarded an Air France plane for my first-ever visit to Mauritania. When I arrived, Diop the driver met me at the airport. Diop's a tall man. A Mauritanian and dressed in his traditional long-flowing robes, he was strikingly impressive. He had been sent by the

German Development Aid Agency to meet me. We said hello and he drove me to the guesthouse where a room had been booked for me.

It was late at night when our car reached the hotel. I was by then extremely tired. As a destination, Mauritania was a new discovery for me. I looked around. I saw that there were not many houses in the area where the hotel was located and they were spaced well apart. What really struck me was the amount of sand. It was everywhere. There was not much vegetation but a lot of sand.

Diop left the car. He approached the cheap-looking zinc door located smack in the middle of a wall behind which the hotel was located. He pressed the doorbell – there was no reply. He banged his fist on the metallic door – in the quiet of the night it sounded like thunder.

Eventually, someone came and opened the door. We followed him onto the hotel's compound and we entered the small house. The hotel clerk told me he would show me my room – I was to follow him. We walked up a narrow flight of stairs. When we arrived on the first floor, we went along a narrow corridor. The whole place was dimly lit. He stopped at the second door to our right.

'We have reserved for you the green room,' he said.

'That's probably appropriate,' I replied.

'The toilet – it's down the corridor, to the left,' he said.

He opened the door and handed me the key.

I thanked him, whereupon he left.

Entering the room I saw that it was sparsely furnished. There was a low double bed to my right. To the left corner I saw a single bed. In the room there was also a desk and drawn curtains next to it. When I walked to the curtains and pushed them aside, I found myself looking into the interior of another room. I closed the curtains.

By now it was way past midnight. I did not like the hotel but there was no other choice. I was thoroughly exhausted and Diop the driver had gone. To unwind after a long flight, I decided I would watch television – but there was no television. *Perhaps I could sit at the desk to read some magazines or the board papers?* I looked at the desk area but it was far too dark to sit there for reading purposes.

I noticed a small table lamp next to the bed. That would be the solution. I switched on the lamp. I sat on the edge of the bed. I took out my documents for the board meeting. Not the most fascinating reading at that time of day but I desperately needed something to read prior to going to bed. I read all the board papers and I made some notes.

Still not able to sleep right away, I looked for something else to occupy my mind. I saw a small document by the bedside. I took the booklet. The front cover, in French, stated that the booklet referred to the *"Maison d'hôtes Jeloua"* – which translated means the "Jeloua Guesthouse".

Opening the booklet I saw that it was a menu of services available at the hotel. The front section provided information on the rooms. The guesthouse had five rooms. They were named after colours: yellow, red, orange, purple and blue. But there was no mention of my room, the green room. How come? The booklet further stated the standard charge was 12,000 um. This standard charge included air conditioning and use of a private bathroom. The booklet mentioned that they had only one green room – at this point my how-come-no-mention-of-my-green-room mystery was solved. The green room, my room, was the cheapest one, at 10,000 um (about thirty US dollars), a real bargain – which further explained why my allotted room was hot and stuffy and why there was no toilet/bathroom nor a television set.

I turned the pages and came to the food section. I could order the "Extra Formula" for 3,000 um – about ten US dollars. Or should I be in a hurry and at the same time wanting something cheaper, there was a proposal for the "African Fast Food Plate" at a mere 1,500 um – about five US dollars. But in case I was in an expansive mood and really wanted to splurge, I could order from the "special orders" section. Within this category, I had some marvellous choices. Lobster was available for 5,000 um – about fifteen US dollars. Or, if I really wanted local fare, I could have delicious camel stew – at the same bargain basement price of 5,000 um.

Having completed my reading of the food section, I turned to the services part of the booklet. I learned that I could order a massage – or I could have my hair braided. I could even order hair removal services.

By now I was thoroughly worn out. I didn't particularly fancy camel stew at one in the morning, nor did I feel any urgent need for my hair to be interlaced. I therefore switched off the lights and went to bed…

22

Dinner Choices

Nouakchott, Mauritania

After attending a board meeting of the Mauritanian Conservation Trust Fund where I was a trustee, I stayed an extra day in Nouakchott. As airfare structures would have it, remaining an additional day had meant a drastic decline in ticket prices, hence my decision. During this day, I spent the entire morning in my hotel room, managing e-mails and returning telephone calls. When lunchtime arrived, I asked the hotel receptionist for suggestions as to where I could go for a meal. I wanted a place accessible by foot but not too far away and where the fare would be local and good.

'I know exactly where you should go,' said the receptionist. And he gave me precise instructions.

I left the hotel and crossed the main road where there was much traffic. Immediately I found the small road that the receptionist had mentioned. It was a sandy road and I walked at a steady pace. Soft sand was everywhere. It was like walking on a beach. Then I found it, the small restaurant recommended. I had arrived at the "Saloon" restaurant.

I walked across the tiny compound in front of the restaurant. There was a vast array of flowers, bright and colourful in their brown clay pots. I passed through the double swing doors – these were cowboy saloon-type swing doors as seen in movies, befitting the name of the restaurant.

The place was empty. I took a seat at one of the corner tables. Almost instantly, the young Mauritanian waitress arrived. She greeted me warmly and handed me the menu. It was a small booklet with a black silhouette design of cowboys and horses on the front cover. The waitress was eager to help but I could see she did not have much experience at serving tables. There were only three items on the menu, so my choice was quickly made.

'I'll have the lamb – and if you can give me a small bottle of mineral water please,' I said to her in French.

49

She dutifully recorded my order. And then, looking up from her notebook and speaking in a gentle, soft and polite voice, she asked me, in French: '*Comment voulez-vous votre viande, bien cuite ou mal cuite?*' "How would you like your meat – well done, or badly done?" she had asked.

23

Bearing Gifts I Come

Dakar, Senegal.

Sitting on the terrace at home, Françoise, our adult son Yann and I were having our lunch. I had just started drinking my soup when Françoise said to Yann:

'Your father's going to Senegal.'

As I travel regularly, such an announcement was by no means exceptional news. For this particular trip, my staff had organised a training meeting for finance managers of some of the WWF countries in western Africa. Senegal had been chosen as the most convenient country for the majority of attendees. My role was to make a presentation there and to have one-to-one meetings with some of the WWF country finance managers.

A few days later, Françoise said, 'About your trip to Senegal.'

'Yes?'

'You know that Yann's girlfriend is Senegalese?'

What was she about to tell me? I had met my son's girlfriend. Yann's a tall six-footer with broad shoulders – a big man by any definition. His girlfriend is a small woman. Together as a couple, they make quite a contrast when they stand together.

'He telephoned earlier today – about your trip,' she said.

'What did he say?'

'He asked if you could bring a few items to Dakar. For his girlfriend's family – her sisters.'

The next day, when I arrived home after work, Françoise said, 'Yann came by today and he left you these two bags.'

I had expected one small parcel – instead, I found myself staring at two large and very full plastic bags. I checked inside. I discovered many items: clothing, women's handbags, toys, dolls, sweets, chocolates and even a few second-hand mobile phones. Looking at the contents of the bundles, I felt uneasy. Had I not been told repeatedly by airport staff not to carry anything on anybody's behalf? Yann had met his girlfriend not that long ago and I did not know her well.

Precautions were therefore called for. I opened both bags. I carefully sorted out all the items, laying them on the floor. One at a time, I looked at every single object. I turned each over and I viewed it from different angles. As to the dolls and stuffed toys, I subjected them to thorough squeezes to ensure nothing was sewn inside. One by one, each object passed my makeshift tests. I packed them into my suitcase – item by item, interspersed between my socks, shirts and office papers.

'And what shall I do with all these when I get there? Did he say I should deliver them to the sisters?'

'No, there's no need. They'll be at the airport.'

The next evening, my plane landed at Léopold Sédar Senghor International Airport, located about twenty miles from Dakar town. The airport was extremely busy when I arrived. Bustling, not so much in terms of planes coming and going but more in terms of the large number of people present there. Making my way through the crowds, I went through passport control. After that, I proceeded to the luggage carousel. I located and picked up my suitcase. Bag in tow and with all the presents inside, I made my way to the exit.

As soon as I went through the main doors of the airport building and onto the open-air compound I felt the warmness of the African evening air. It was a pleasant sensation. There were even more people lingering outside the airport than inside. How would I recognize the sisters? I supposed they would come to me. It should be easy for them to find me. Being tall and Chinese, I certainly stood out.

But there were no sisters approaching me. Neither was there a WWF-welcome-to-my-country-person. *What should I do? Just stand there in the middle of the night, amidst the throng of people and wait? Or perhaps I'd better grab a taxi and head for the hotel? But then what would I do with the gifts?*

Then the solution dawned on me. Of course, I only need to use my mobile phone to call Yann for the telephone numbers of the sisters. I switched it on. As I started to dial Switzerland, two young Senegalese women came up to me.

'You must be Yann's father,' said one of them.

'Yes.'

I greeted them and we shook hands.

'Well, in this bag I have the items from your sister.'

We were having our conversation standing in the airport's exterior compound – an area where there were no tables. No tables but a lot of people. I squatted down in order to open my suitcase. The sisters also squatted to join me. Laying the suitcase flat on the ground, I opened it.

There I was, late in the night, an open suitcase on the floor – with two young women squatted beside me. I sifted through my clothes and handed, one by one, assorted items to them. Whilst I was doing that, two of my male WWF colleagues arrived. They had come to pick me up. Seeing me as described, they were taken aback and unsure as to how to react. Hesitant and somewhat embarrassed, they just stood there – frozen.

Aware they might easily misinterpret what was happening, I quickly stood up.

'Hello gents. Thanks for coming. Meet the sisters of my son's girlfriend. I'm delivering some items to them,' I said.

Instantly, big smiles flashed on the faces of my welcoming committee – thoroughly relieved that all was above board. The sisters thanked me for having delivered the presents. I took my leave and we proceeded to my hotel…

24

More Fish

Stone Town, Zanzibar

Zanzibar consists of a group of islands located to the east of continental Africa. The city's historic town, known as Stone Town, is a World Heritage site. Zanzibar's not a country. It forms part of the United Republic of Tanzania. In Arabic, its name means "Land of the Blacks". Coined from the Arabic terms *"zinj"* for black and *"barr"* for land.

I was scheduled to visit the WWF Tanzania head office situated in Dar es Salaam and one of the field project offices located in Zanzibar. The goal was to review financial systems and to help advise the country manager concerning the hiring of his finance manager.

'The only way to get there is via Dar,' an African colleague said to me.

By "Dar" he was referring to Dar es Salaam, the capital of Tanzania.

'What you can do is first visit our Dar office and then, after that, schedule Zanzibar.'

'I see. Thanks for the info,' I said.

My plane landed at Julius Nyerere International Airport in Dar es Salaam. A WWF Tanzania colleague met me and we drove to the hotel. After I had completed the hotel's check-in procedures, we decided to lunch together. We headed to the hotel's poolside area. The pool was small and there was a bar area with three high stools next to it. No one was sitting on any of them. On one side of the pool were deckchairs and long chairs faced the ocean on the other side of the pool. Not far from the bar area were a few small round metal tables with some chairs scattered around them. We occupied the first table, the one nearest to us. The sun was shining. The sky was clear.

'What a beautiful ocean,' I said.

'Yes, but there's a problem,' my colleague said.

'Meaning?' I asked.

The waiter came. We were handed menus.

'Let's order first,' my colleague said.

We studied the menu.

'Lobsters are not expensive here,' I said.

I ordered grilled lobster and a cold beer.

'But what's this problem you were referring to?' I asked again.

My colleague pointed at the ocean.

'Beneath what you see – the blue waters of this ocean – there's not much going on. Corals have been destroyed. Fish have been killed. It's because of years of dynamite fishing. Just imagine, explosions underwater. Not only fish: all other sea life has been indiscriminately destroyed. A real shame – but this has happened.'

'What a pity,' I said.

'And as you know, the public is not always aware of the problem. Pollution and environmental damage underwater is invisible.'

'I know. Alfred Nobel invented dynamite but I'm not sure it was such a good idea. No doubt we have the Nobel prizes today – but his invention must have done much harm,' I said.

Over the next two days I spent time at the Dar offices and had various financial meetings and reviews. On the third day it was time to leave Dar. A driver picked me up and we headed for the airport. At the airport, there were people everywhere; a scene I had become accustomed to at African airports. Tanzania has a population of more than forty million – and as one would expect, much of that population is concentrated in the towns. As a result, Dar airport was very busy. By contrast, Zanzibar, where I was headed, is a relatively sparsely populated place, with just under a million inhabitants.

As our small propeller-driven plane took off for Zanzibar, I read up on Zanzibar history. I learnt that its historic capital, Stone Town, was at one time the capital of an Omani sultanate. I became aware of the Arab traders and the slave trade. I could imagine the bazaars and the spices. Eventually, my plane landed at Zanzibar and I was driven directly to the WWF offices.

Our car approached an impressively large three-storeyed detached house situated within an extensive garden full of tall mature trees.

'It's huge, this place. This can't be our offices?' I said.

'It is – but we only rent three rooms at the back,' Harry my driver replied.

'I see.'

'Did you know that Dr Livingstone used to stay here?' he said.

'Is that right? I never realised he came to Zanzibar. I thought he only travelled within mainland Africa.'

Harry drove the car to the back portion of the house. He parked it near a small door. We left the car and entered the office.

We did not stay long there. I greeted the two WWF staff working there and Harry picked up some papers that he needed.

'Now we go to Stone Town for a quick lunch,' said Harry.

'OK, let's do that,' I said.

'We will meet the project manager there. Then we go together to the project site,' he said.

'Sounds fine to me.'

As we were driving to town, I was told that Livingstone did indeed stay in Zanzibar, although not for a long period. After his death, he was buried in England, but his heart remained in Africa.

'He left his heart in Africa – but I don't mean it in the romantic sense,' Harry said.

'I don't get it,' I said.

'When he died, his crew removed all the insides of his body – including his heart. His body was then dried and shipped to England. He's now buried in Westminster Abbey. But his heart- they buried it in Africa.'

'How interesting.'

Our car arrived at Stone Town. It was a quiet place. There were not many vehicles or people to be seen anywhere. The buildings were low and mostly white. As we walked along the town's narrow lanes, I admired the beauty of the buildings. Many of them were built in the 19th century and had elaborately decorated wooden doors.

'All buildings here are made of stone,' said Harry.

We walked through some narrow cobble-stoned streets till we reached a narrow alley that sloped steeply downwards. I took care not to slip. We went down that passageway. We entered a tiny café. It looked like the only possible place for a meal.

In the dining area of the restaurant, along the wall, was a fridge with double see-through doors. Different soft drinks were on display. Next to it were five small round tables. We occupied the one by the fridge. I looked at the small typed menu that had been placed in the middle of our table.

'I'll have the grilled chicken,' I said to the waiter when he arrived.

'Sorry, no grilled chicken today,' he said.

He spoke English, not Swahili. But he did not have my chicken. I ordered lamb.

'Sorry, no lamb,' he said.

I gave up. I asked him what he proposed.

I ended up ordering boiled octopus cooked with spices.

As we were finishing our lunch, the expected colleague, the project manager, arrived. We had coffee and then together we left the restaurant, got into the car and proceeded with our drive to the coast, to where the WWF project was located. As we were driving in the car, I enquired about the project.

'Your environmental education project – for how many people are you responsible?' I asked the project manager.

'You mean how many people report to me?' he said.

'No – I mean how many people do you educate,' I said.

'Thousands.'

'You mean hundreds?'

'No, thousands.'

'That's a lot of people. I don't see how you can do that,' I said.

'I talk to the village chiefs and they in turn talk to the villagers.'

'I see. And what do you specifically educate them on?'

'Dynamite fishing.'

I became all ears.

'It's a big problem. For some of the fishermen, it's an easy way to fish. They only need to throw a few sticks into the water. An explosion occurs – and up float the fish. They only see the fish, not the environmental damage. Nor the fact that they are killing the smaller fish that will never mature.'

'The villagers – do they listen to you?' I asked.

'Yes. But sometimes it gets difficult.'

'Why?'

'In extreme cases, the villagers do not listen – they remain convinced fishing this way is OK.'

'Why's that so?'

'They believe that when it next rains more fish will come…'

25

Entry Formalities

City "x", Africa
(The city is not named as I do not wish to
have problems should I re-visit the country)

Laurent Somé telephoned me. He called because he wanted help from me. Some problems had recently arisen, including another case whereby substantial sums had been misappropriated by one of his country managers.

I found myself again flying to Africa. Arriving at the destination's airport I joined the queue in front of the border guard. I reached for my passport; fumbling inside my black sling "computer" bag, I found it. I rechecked the stamps of my entry visa even though I knew I had it, having obtained the visa only two days before. I looked once again inside my bag. This time I took out my yellow vaccination booklet – the document where all the necessary jabs had been recorded: yellow fever, typhoid, plus a few others.

Entry papers sorted, with dusk approaching, I proceeded with my self-invented whilst-in-Africa anti-malaria ritual. I took out my plastic bottle of mosquito repellent – a small red bottle, equipped with a black manual pump. Before embarking on my trip, I had enquired at a chemist and the Swiss pharmacist had shown me multiple coloured bottles of spray. When told I was heading for Africa, she had recommended her most potent bottle: the red one.

I started by giving my arms a generous spray. I sprayed my trousers. Although mosquitoes do bite on the face and neck, I had no intention of spraying myself directly on the face. Instead, I raised the bottle high above my head. Then I gave the bottle two strong squirts, after which I waited. The tiny particles in the air slowly descended upon me. It was like being anointed. It did not smell bad, rather the scent was that of a cheap perfume.

It came my turn to present my travel documents. I found myself standing in front of a surly border guard. Sitting behind his narrow glass cubicle, he glared at me. He did not return my "good evening" greeting. He took my passport, turned it open and looked at my photograph. He then raised his head to glance at me. Having ensured that face and photograph matched, he flipped through my passport's pages. He stopped at the page where the entry visa was stamped. The visa alone took up an entire page of my passport. He tried to find something wrong with my papers. He went through my passport pages yet again, re-examining the page where my photograph was. When I thought that he was about to give up, he spoke to me.

'Your yellow vaccination booklet?' he said, in French.

I gave him the yellow booklet. He treated me to a repeat performance of his "My friend, I'll-try-to-find-something-wrong-with-your-papers" act. Eventually, he gave up. Reluctantly, he returned my travel documents. Without a word but with a dismissive wave of his hand, he indicated I could finally enter the country.

I left him and walked towards the baggage collection area. I had hardly advanced three paces when I was again stopped. A bulky African official, dressed in military uniform, placed himself squarely in my path.

'Good evening, sir – your passport please,' he demanded loudly.

'But… I just showed it to your colleague,' I tried to protest, as I pointed to the cubicle behind me.

'Your passport please,' he repeated, in a low voice.

Apparently he did not want to hear about my comments concerning his colleague.

'But who are you?' I said.

'Airport security.'

'Can I have proof?'

He slid his big right hand into his beige safari jacket pocket. Out came an official looking identification card – complete with photograph. Confidently holding card in hand, he showed it to me. I read the document. I decided I'd better give up.

'Here you are,' I said, handing him my passport.

He took my passport and he flipped through the pages.

'Can I see your invitation please?'

'Invitation?'

I pretended I did not know what he meant. But I knew he was referring to the invitation I had received from the WWF country office. For some countries visas need to be substantiated with invitations from contacts in host countries. It looked like I was in one such country.

'I no longer have it. I had to attach the invitation to my visa application. Look, I have the entry visa in my passport.'

'Sorry, but you must also show an invitation. Either the original or even a photocopy.'

'But the visa – it's supposed to be an entry visa.'

'Sorry, it's the rule. Please see my colleagues outside,' he said.

'Colleagues outside?'

'First go pick up your bags. Then proceed to the customs office outside the airport building. Ask anyone and someone will tell you where to go.'

With those words, he walked off – with my passport still in his possession.

I uttered some swear words but was careful that they were only audible to myself.

I arrived at the baggage collection area. Many bags came through but not mine. After what seemed an eternity, my bag finally appeared on the carousel. My well-travelled bag in tow, I left the baggage collection area.

With relief, I saw the friendly face of a WWF representative – the driver. We shook hands.

'My passport's been confiscated. So where's this customs office outside the airport?' I said.

'I know it. We have first to exit the airport building. It's on the other side of the car park. Follow me.'

A short walk and we were in front of the small building that housed the officials. We entered and found ourselves in a tiny room. The walls were dirty and the paint was peeling. The place was sparsely furnished and what was there looked like it had seen better days. At one corner of the room was a wooden desk. Behind it sat a small uniformed man. He was elderly and judging by his manners and by the elaborateness of his uniform, he was a senior official. The room was dim as there was only one light source: a naked light bulb dangling on a wire from the ceiling. At the other corner of the room was a second desk directly facing the first one. Behind it sat a younger official – and like the airport security person I had previously encountered, he was a big man. He looked distinctly menacing.

The elderly official pointed to three small chairs lined up alongside a wall. We were to sit there whilst we waited for our turn. This was because the younger official was occupied – he was busy addressing the two young men sitting meekly in front of his desk. We took our seats as instructed.

'I hear you. Yes, I understand. Yes, you are Canadian students. Yes, you have no money – but you still need a visa. Rules are rules,' said the younger official.

Neither Canadian replied.

The official continued, this time in a you-better-do-what-I-say tone.

'I'm sorry but you must have a visa. It's only fifty dollars. I have no more application forms but I can make photocopies.'

He glared at the Canadians. At the other end of the room, behind his desk, the senior official looked on impassively. The Canadians did not reply. They shifted in their chairs. Biding his time, the younger official looked at them as he waited, like a hunter closing in on its prey.

Then one of the Canadians looked at his travelling companion. Ever so slightly, the second man nodded.

'OK,' softly said the first man.

The official stood up. He went to the photocopy machine and made two copies of the visa application form. He gave them to the visitors. Subdued and beaten in the unfair tug-of-war, they silently filled in the forms. They paid the official. He took the cash and he put it into his desk drawer. He scribbled something on the copies of the official application forms, presumably his signature – these also ended up in his drawer. I could only speculate what might later happen to those forms and to the cash.

He stamped the two passports and returned them to the young visitors. Wearily, the two Canadians stood up.

'Thank you,' said one of them.

His "thank you" remark surprised me.

Then they left.

With the official's two "customers" gone, it was now my turn.

He looked my way and pointed to the vacated chairs. We were to sit there. Time for some interrogation – unless I pay up.

We sat in front of him. The elderly official at the other end of the room continued to utter not a word but was observing all proceedings.

The younger official held my passport high in his hand. He showed it to me.

'Your passport?' he said.

'Yes.'

'You have a visa. But you also need an invitation.'

'It's with your visa office in Switzerland.'

He did not reply. Silence – as he stared at me.

'For whom do you work?' he said.

His colleague continued to look on.

'WWF,' I replied.

It did not seem to ring any bells in his head.

'We have authorisation from the Ministry,' the driver said.

'Show it to me.'

'I don't have it on me,' the driver said.

'Then how do I know it's true?'

'It's in the car.'

'Can you get it?'

'OK,' said the driver.

He stood up and left the room.

And there I was, alone with the two officials. A cat and mouse game: two cats, with me, the mouse. The three of us waited. They did not say anything. I behaved like them. I said nothing. It was a peculiar silence. I checked my mobile phone for messages. There were none.

Many minutes later, the driver returned. He handed the copy of the authorization document to the younger official who started to read the letter. I could see the document had various signatures and official-looking stamps on it.

He muttered something in local language to the older official.

All of a sudden, he stood up.

'Sir! Welcome to our country. I thank you for taking the time to be here. We are so glad you have come,' he said.

Simultaneously, his boss, who had previously just sat there motionless, actually moved. He rushed over to me.

'Sir, we are really so sorry to have kept you waiting. Please do accept our apologies,' he said.

The younger official politely returned my passport to me. The driver and I started to leave and as we were doing so, both the officials rushed to open the door for us.

The senior official held the door wide open and with exaggerated deference, he and his colleague bade the driver and myself goodbye.

Ah, what a difference a few ministerial signatures on a piece of paper can make…

26

Midnight Fun

Lofoten Islands, Norway

Puffins have an amusing appearance. They are colourful birds with large beaks and they look as though they have come straight out of a comic book. A seabird species, puffins feed primarily by diving for fish – although they do eat other sea creatures, squid being one example. These small birds can also be found in the Lofoten Islands, located way up north, in fact within the Arctic Circle, in Norway.

I was attending a WWF annual conference, as well as the organisation's board and executive committee meetings in Norway. I had arrived in the morning, the Sunday before the meetings were due to start. That Sunday afternoon, I joined some colleagues and together we boarded a medium-sized Norwegian fishing boat so that we could go view puffins. Our boat went out to sea and not long after, it approached a small rocky island. It was an island inhabited by puffins. I saw a colony. As we observed them from our boat, some of them in turn looked back at us. There were hundreds of birds gathered. They stood on the hill, a barren rock of an island – that can best be described as a mini Gibraltar. They were mostly gathered towards the top so that the entire place looked like a large ice cream cone with standing puffins for topping.

Following the "puffin" Sunday boat trip, our meetings commenced the next day. During the latter part of the afternoon, once we had participated in quite a few discussion sessions, a colleague made an announcement.

'Dinner's at eight this evening – the bus will leave at seven-thirty. Please be at the reception area on time,' he said.

The appointed time arrived. My colleagues and I gathered at the hotel's reception area. As the place was tiny, it soon became crowded and we spilled over onto the hotel's exterior compound. We did not have long to wait before our buses arrived. We boarded the buses and as my bus left the hotel, I observed it was light, even though it was evening. It was the Nordic summer.

We arrived at a quaint Norwegian restaurant located in a building painted in a brownish cum burgundy-red colour. Together with its bluish-grey roof, the house had a colour scheme typical of the region. Although the restaurant was large, we filled it. I do not now remember what we had for dinner – but do recall speeches were delivered, including the customary "thank you" (for our dinner) comments acknowledging corporate sponsors. During the meal we not only ate, we also sipped wine. As the evening progressed, further dinner conversation was accompanied by increased wine drinking. Given that it was dinnertime and no one had to drive home, a "bit" of wine seemed a good idea then.

At around 11 p.m., a colleague proceeded to the front of the room.

'Ladies and gentlemen, I hope you have enjoyed the evening. I know it's getting late, perhaps even past bedtime for some of you. Normally we would be returning to the hotel. In fact the buses are here. However, I've a better idea. Tomorrow's programme includes whale watching. But there's a problem – severe storms are expected. That would not make it the ideal time to go to sea,' he said.

'What do you suggest?' someone at the back of the room asked.

'Friends, this is the land of the midnight sun. It's late but as you can see, it's light outside. Yes, it's stormy this evening – but only slightly so. Tomorrow is when it will really blow. So sailing's out for tomorrow. But this evening – that's a possibility. I've already checked with the captains of two boats. If you agree, I suggest we go whale watching tonight.'

Spurred on by the after-effects of wine and mutual encouragement, it seemed a good idea. Whale watching at night in the land of the midnight sun. *How many chances in my life will I get to do something as adventurous as this?*

And so, with food heavy in my stomach, wine in my head, I joined colleagues and we boarded the buses. Our vehicles headed for the harbour. Upon arrival, we embarked onto two large boats. Within minutes the sailors had unhooked the boats' moorings. Our vessels started to shift and slide sideways, away from the quay. I recall Prince Philip standing on the deck of one of the boats, the bigger of the two. He had joined the conference in his capacity as President of WWF International. I was with other colleagues on a different boat. The two boats left port and we sailed off to the open sea. As we did so, I looked at the sea. The waters were slightly choppy but nothing dramatic. As our boat went further out to sea, the waves began to rise higher and higher. At the same time the winds blew ever stronger – whilst the skies continued to darken. I had a feeling of impending doom. Then, minutes later, it hit us. The horrid storm we did not expect arrived with incredible force. Strong winds whipped our boat whilst heavy rain poured down. The agitated sea rocked our boat violently to and fro. The well-intended sailing journey had turned into a living nightmare. A colleague announced the sighting of whale fins in the far distance as some had whales dived – but I was no longer interested. The skies darkened even more ominously and the seas became rougher. As our boat continued to sway, the dinner I had just eaten returned to haunt me, as did the wine. I felt dizzy. So as to not fall over, I gripped the boat's railings. I could feel my head swirling and I felt nauseous. I decided to make my way down to the lower decks.

'Where are you going?' a friendly voice asked me.

I could not even find the strength to reply. Slowly, very slowly, whilst clutching my stomach at the same time, I headed down towards the hull. I just wanted to crawl into a corner and die – or at least to suffer quietly by myself whilst waiting for the trip to end. Step by slow painful step, I descended the stairs. As I arrived at the hull, I saw that many other passengers had already preceded me. I do not recall how many hours we spent in the hull, but it seemed an eternity.

Finally the time came for the boat to turn around. It returned to port – and my ordeal ended. All my hull-class travelling companions and I could barely muster the energy to crawl out and disembark. We boarded the bus. We returned to the hotel and there I slumped onto my waiting bed.

Waking the next day, I looked out the window. It was a glorious morning and the sun shone golden and bright. Observing the leaves on the trees, I could see there was a slight breeze blowing – a perfect whale-watching sailing day…

27

'Dr Livingstone, I Presume?'

London, England

Invited, I went to London to give a presentation on socially responsible investments. As the presentation occurred on a Friday, I decided to stay the weekend with my sister in Hampstead. On Saturday morning I took the tube (the London Underground) to go to Westminster Abbey. I wanted to see exactly where Livingstone was buried. Upon arrival, I was confronted by an impressive Gothic-style building. The place was immense and the cathedral was a beauty to look at. I followed the signs and joined the queuing crowd. I entered the famous place founded over a thousand years ago – where William the Conqueror was crowned in 1066.

Once inside the cathedral I was immediately struck by the height of the ceilings. There were many visitors but it did not take me long to come across abbey staff. It was anyway impossible not to see them. They were all dressed in eye-catching medieval-style gowns of distinctively bright colours: red, green and blue.

I approached a male staff member.

'Would you know where Livingstone's buried?' I asked.

'Yes, he's just over there – come with me.'

I followed him. After a few paces, he stopped. He looked down at the floor.

'Strange – I was sure he was buried here. I must have mixed him up with someone else. Trouble is – there are so many of them,' he said.

'How many?'

'Oh, I don't know – maybe five thousand.'

'Oh, wow!'

'I'll look it up for you.'

He checked his hand-held electronic device.

'Ah, I see. Yes, he's over there – on the other side, at the nave. Let me show you on the map.'

'Thanks.'

I left him. I did the tourist bit. I walked along the recommended route, following the instructions exactly as per the guide map handed to me. I listened attentively to my audio player. I looked at the various marble-white statues. I passed the shrine of Edward the Confessor, so-called because of his deep piety. I saw the tomb of Elizabeth I, the Virgin Queen. There was the tomb of Mary Queen of Scots – also known as Mary Stuart. I passed many others. At one part of the cathedral I came across a grouping of statues. That was unusual as most of the other statues were individual ones. One of them depicted William Shakespeare – even though his body's actually not in the abbey.

How would Livingstone's tomb be marked? Would it be grouped with other tombs? Surely there would not be a statue of him alone? The place seemed to be reserved mostly for kings and queens – although the abbey's website does mention "kings, queens, statesmen and soldiers; poets, priests, heroes and villains." There I was, looking for Livingstone – as did Stanley over a hundred years ago. But mine was by far an easier task. I need not search across Africa.

An hour and about a hundred odd statues later, I arrived at the nave area. Time to look for Livingstone – but just as I arrived there, a voice broke out over the speaker system.

'Ladies and gentlemen, this abbey is a place of worship. Every hour, we observe a minute of silence for prayers. If we may ask you to now please remain silent.'

I hurriedly walked two paces to observe some floor writings I had noticed in the middle of the nave. Might as well find something to read whilst observing the mandatory minute of silence. I looked down and saw two large rectangular stone plaques. Placed one next to the other, each was about three-foot wide and seven-foot long. I read what was written on the one to my right.

On the floor was the following inscription:

"Brought by faithful hands over land and sea here rests David Livingstone, missionary, traveller, philanthropist. Born March 19, 1813 at Blantyre, Lanarkshire, died May 1, 1873 at Chitambo's

Village, Ulala. For 30 years his life was spent in an unwearied effort to evangelize the native races, to explore the undiscovered secrets, to abolish the desolating slave trade of Central Africa, where with his last words, he wrote, "All I can add in my solitude, is, may heaven's rich blessing come down on every one, American, English or Turk, who will help to heal this open sore of the world.""

The minute of silence lapsed. I left the abbey. As I joined the moving crowds at Westminster tube station, I remembered the house in Tanzania, the building where Livingstone once lived and that his heart had remained in Africa…

28

Edmund Hillary

Montreux, Switzerland

Mount Everest peaks at an altitude of close to 9,000 metres – it's the highest mountain on Earth. The first men to ascend it were Edmund Hillary and Sherpa Tenzing Norgay. That was in 1953.

I had read about the conquest of Everest when I was in high school. A page of my geography book had a black and white photograph – it showed Edmund Hillary and Sherpa Tenzing, both wearing goggles. I had marvelled at the fact it was at all possible to climb such a high mountain.

'I'm really pleased to meet you,' I said to Edmund, just before we sat down. We were both attending a conference in Montreux, a small Swiss lakeside town. During the lunch break, I found myself seated next to my schooldays' textbook hero.

Born in 1920, Edmund passed away in 2008. A New Zealander, he was a tall and handsome person. Stature-wise, he was like the actor Gregory Peck. He looked very fit. He was friendly and articulate. That was a surprise for me as I had a misconception – previously, my image of mountain climbers had been that they were solitary and reclusive individuals, and hence not very communicative. Edmund communicated well. He was likeable and I enjoyed chatting with him.

He told me about Everest and about how some mountaineers had been behaving badly – leaving rubbish and other items behind them.

'At one time there was even a crashed helicopter abandoned there,' he said.

It was all news to me. I had not known such problems existed. As lunch ended and we were having coffee I said, 'When you climbed Everest, you spent days getting there. And finally you arrived – what did you do when you were up there?'

'We admired the view – planted the Union Jack. After fifteen minutes, with our oxygen running low, we had to start our descent.'

From Edmund, I had food for thought about life and many related issues. Often it's not solely the destination that counts – the journey's just as important too…

29

Have Cash Will Travel

Gland, Switzerland

Sitting at the rectangular conference table in my office, Betty Lynn Evans and I had just finished reviewing financial statements. Betty Lynn's a Canadian citizen who has lived for many years in Switzerland. A chartered accountant, she knows financial matters well. After we had completed our review of the financial statements, she brought up another subject. I had my doubts as to whether I would approve her proposals.

'But we have to do it this way,' she protested. 'The problem is that there are no banks in Georgia. And it's especially so where our project is located. That's why Luc says he has to take cash.'

Luc Deslarze was one of the project managers. He's European and he sports a moustache.

'I'd like to talk to him,' I said.

This was during the early days when Eastern Europe was starting to open up. Luc was the conservation project manager for Georgia. He had contacted the finance department because he wanted to carry cash to Georgia. As the standard procedures did not allow for the transportation of significant amounts of money by employees, he needed my authorisation.

Betty Lynn telephoned Luc. She asked him to join us.

Within minutes Luc arrived at my office. We exchanged some friendly conversation.

'I really don't like the idea,' I said.

'I don't like it either but it's the only way for our projects to receive funds.'

'And what if I don't agree?'

'That would be bad news. With no funds, we'll have to close projects. And even if we do that – staff will still have to be paid for work already done.'

'I see.'

'But don't worry. I've carried cash in the past. No doubt the amounts were small but I've done it before.'

'What about your safety? People get killed for even smaller sums.'

'I'll not walk along dark alleys at night.'

I saw that there was no practical alternative possible.

'OK, I agree,' I said. 'But please, not a word to anyone. I don't want this temporary fix to become a widespread habit,' I added.

'Sure, I'll be discreet.'

As Luc started to leave, a question popped up in my mind.

'By the way – how will you transport the cash? Not in a bulging wallet?' I said.

'Of course not.'

'Well then?'

'Well hidden – in my socks.'

'Talk about smelly money…'

30

Pampas BBQ

Buenos Aires, Argentina

Have you ever been to Argentina? Visited the Pampas and had a barbecue there? Experienced wining and dining in the moonlight? That must be something marvellous. I have seen it in cowboy movies. Scenes of extensive ranches set amidst wide-open spaces. Burning firewood would make crackling sounds. Gauchos would be strumming guitars. Nearby, meat on iron spikes would be roasting, turning slowly over hot coals. Guests would be eating, drinking, chatting and laughing – generally feeling cheerful and having a good time. Ah, this would be"The South American Way".

As I had never been to Buenos Aires before, I was excited to arrive there. My trip's programme included the WWF annual conference, various other meetings (for example, the WWF International Board and WWF International Executive Committee meetings), as well as a fundraising event. The city reminded me of Madrid in Spain.

After I had checked in at the hotel, I entered my assigned room. I read the small pile of documents that reception had handed me. Included in the pack was a stack of invitations for the week – for lunch, for cocktails and for dinners. One of the invitations caught my eye. What attracted me was not the ornate invitation card itself, nor was it the name of the important guest of honour. What struck me were the timings written on the card. It informed that guests had to be ready to board the buses at 5.30 p.m. Cocktails were to start at 7.30 p.m. This would be followed by dinner, sponsored by some Argentinean corporations, at 8.00 p.m.

A bus pickup at 5.30 p.m. and cocktails at 7.30 p.m. meant a two-hour drive. It looked like we would be going to the wide-open spaces of the Pampas. I found it very exciting – finally it had come, my chance to experience the South American barbecue.

The four coaches arrived on time. My colleagues and I, together with other guests, filled up the various vehicles. Our bus left the hotel compound. I saw that my fellow passengers were in a jovial mood and we admired the sights as our bus navigated the busy city roads. As there was much traffic, our bus moved slowly. We passed important buildings and famous monuments. There was the Obelisk of Buenos Aires, built to commemorate the 400th anniversary of the founding of the city – famous because a huge condom had once been placed over it in support of an Aids campaign. Another landmark was the Buenos Aires Recoleta cemetery. It is in there that Eva Peron is buried. The cemetery is unusual in that its layout is like a small town – complete with tree-lined paths and elaborate mausoleums.

We continued driving past more landmarks. Half an hour later, we encountered serious after-office traffic. Our bus slowed down even further. Our motoring speed decreased to a snail's pace. Despite the heavy traffic all vehicles were nevertheless moving – although only merely inching along. Eventually, after an exasperatingly long ride, we reached our destination. Our bus pulled into a bleak-looking car park that was next to a mundane communal town hall. I looked at my watch and I understood. A fair amount of time had been planned for the bus ride. The reason was not for the purpose of heading out to the Pampas – but rather, for manoeuvring in the traffic jams.

I was most thankful to get out, to stretch my legs. We descended the bus. We were directed to the town hall building. The cocktail reception did not last long as our buses had arrived late. After a couple of welcome drinks, we took our seats and were served dinner. I was hungry by then. The dinner was OK but it was certainly no moonlight Pampas barbecue.

Have you ever had a barbecue in the moonlight, in the Pampas? No? Me neither…

31

On Wheels

Quito, Ecuador

The capital city of Quito is San Francisco de Quito – often called by its shorter name of "Quito". It's a sprawling town located on the eastern slopes of Pichincha, an active volcano in the Andes Mountains – where there are many active volcanoes, including the Cotopaxi.

Attending various WWF meetings, I was staying at the Hilton Colon Quito hotel. The hotel's a short walk from the colonial old town, a UNESCO World Heritage site. One lunchtime, having already had a few meals at the hotel, I decided to go in search of something different. It was midday and it was a sunny but it was not hot – this is because Quito is located at roughly 3,000 metres above sea level.

I left the hotel and after a short walk I came across a small local eatery. It had an outdoor terrace and it seemed the perfect place to taste local food and to observe Quito street life. I decided to try it. On the terrace an elderly couple occupied one of the four small tables. Seated by the restaurant's entrance, they stared at me but did not say anything.

I settled for a table at the edge of the terrace close by the road. I pulled up the cleanest chair I could see and sat myself down. Although I speak no Spanish, when the waiter came we somehow managed to muddle through the ordering process. It was a peaceful and calm Sunday. On and off, a car would appear and slowly cruise by. Apart from the occasional passing vehicle, it was otherwise quiet and uneventful.

The waiter returned with the lunch I had ordered – cobs of Andean corn with Ecuadorian moist cheese. It looked and smelled good. I started to eat what he had brought but I simply could not finish the huge helping. I stopped eating. I placed my knife and fork on my plate. Then, at that same instant, I heard it. It was a loud sound – emitted by metallic wheels rolling furiously on the terrace's concrete floor.

It took her a split second to arrive. Suddenly she was next to me, very close, right beside my chair. The woman had long black hair and her head was at the same level as my chest. She had a torso and arms but was legless. She was on a square wooden platform that had been fitted with four wheels. With her body placed firmly in the middle of the structure and using her arms as powerful oars pushing on the ground, she had propelled herself at breakneck speed to be next to me.

With pleading eyes, she looked at me as she pointed to my unfinished plate. I understood but was unsure what to do. Would the café owner allow me to hand her the food? Looking for help, I glanced at the waiter who was standing nearby. To my relief, he nodded. I handed her my plate and the cutlery. With both hands she accepted the plate. She said something I did not understand, probably a thank you. Then, as quickly as she had come – with her strong arms pushing against the floor and with another loud roar of rolling wheels- she propelled herself back to the corner of the terrace from where she had come.

Thoroughly shaken, I returned to the hotel. In the end, it was not a quiet and uneventful Sunday lunch. I had experienced much more of Quito street life than I had initially bargained for…

32

Kofi Annan's Fountain Pen

Beijing, China

I was in Beijing attending a WWF annual conference and the board meeting of trustees where I had to make a presentation on the finances of WWF. Whilst there, one evening I walked into the hotel's bar to see who was already there. I found Ste Drayton, not at the bar's counter but sitting in a corner of the room. I joined him.

Ste's British. He's an information technology specialist. His forename is either Steve or Steven or Stephan but everyone calls him Ste. As long as I can recall, he's Ste. I said hello to him and asked about his day.

The waitress arrived.

'I'll have another beer,' said Ste.

'Give me the same,' I said.

As we chatted, other colleagues came into the room and soon there were eight of us.

We occupied the single available sofa and the half dozen armchairs that encircled a coffee table. There was the usual exchange of news concerning the day's proceedings, about what went satisfactorily and what did not and regarding how some of the WWF colleagues had behaved well, or not. Then we discussed the city's air pollution, which seemed to be reducing.

'It's due to the time of the year,' a colleague said.

Another colleague contributed to the discussions.

'It gets really bad in spring. If you come during springtime you'll find sandstorms. They are frequent during that time of the year. The sand would have come all the way from the Gobi Desert,' he said.

Sitting with us was Paul Steele. Paul was at that time the Chief Operating Officer – the "COO" (pronounced in almost the same way as the sound emitted by pigeons). Paul's British. Paul used to work for Richard Branson's Virgin Group.

'Paul, how was your day?' Ste said.

Someone laughed.

'Paul, you *must* tell them what happened,' the colleague said.

'OK, I will. Kofi Annan came to Beijing at our request.' Paul paused. Ste took another gulp of beer, drinking directly from the bottle. I drank some of mine.

'I was appointed head of our three-man team. We had been seconded to accompany Kofi for official discussions. So we duly picked him up at his hotel and went by car to attend the meeting.'

I pictured in my head an official-looking black sedan cruising silently along Beijing streets.

'At the venue, we met the Chinese VIPs. As they entered the conference room we noticed they came with three other people. They looked like assistants. At first we were unsure why they were there but as soon as the discussions started, it became obvious.'

'Why were they there?' an impatient soul asked.

'You need to imagine the scene. On one side of the conference table sat our team of three, with myself sitting alongside Kofi. Across the table sat the officials together with the three assistants. And what happened was that each time one of the officials said something, anything, the three assistants would furiously take notes. They were writing as though their lives depended on it. And whenever Kofi spoke, it was the same – the three assistants noted everything down.'

'On our side, did anyone take notes?' I asked

'No, nobody did.'

'The officials were not offended?' Ste asked.

'As the Chinese talked, Kofi continued to listen – maintaining constant eye contact. Then, without a single glance at me, he discreetly extended his right arm in my direction. Held in his hand was his Mont Blanc fountain pen.'

We all laughed.

'I took his Mont Blanc. And from that moment – each time anybody uttered the slightest word – there were the six of us, scribbling away…'

33

'Veni, Vidi, Vici'

Jakarta, Indonesia

Early one morning I was sitting in my new (I had since been "promoted", moving from my "cubicle" to a proper office) office in Gland, in Switzerland, reading my e-mails, when Gillian D'Souza, my secretary, walked in. Gillian's British and she has impeccable English grammar and a clipped British accent.

'Good morning,' she said.

I returned the greeting.

'How was the trip? How did it go?' she asked

She was referring to my trip to Indonesia. I had helped the internal auditor with his Jakarta audit.

'Excellent – everything went smoothly. It was a good week.'

'You found time to enjoy the local food?'

'Yes I did – and I must tell you about a meal I had. It was during the last evening.'

'Tell me,' she said.

'Iskandar's one of the project managers. He invited his team members and myself for dinner and he took us to his favourite local restaurant. It was located along a busy street where there were many other restaurants. The dimly lit place had a zinc roof but no walls.'

'I see, a fancy place,' Gillian said.

'As we entered, I noticed multiple rows of long wooden tables with benches on both sides.'

'So?'

'Iskandar's someone who holds himself upright. Proud and confident, he exudes assurance. When I first saw him with his team, it was clear he was the boss. But let me come back to the dinner.

At the restaurant, he was the first to reach our table. As he arrived there,

80

he immediately stretched out his right arm. Across the table, in one majestic movement, he swept his arm upwards, from left to right – as a conqueror might do before announcing "I, Caesar, have arrived".'

'And why would he do that?' she said.

'The instant he did that all hell broke loose. The entire surface of the oily table instantly trembled, bursting alive. A zillion spindly legs – attached to an army of brown cockroaches hastily propelled their anxious owners away in all directions of the compass.'

Would you like the name of a great eating place?

34

Dive Bomber

Tokyo, Japan

I was invited to make a presentation in Tokyo – this was for the Triple Bottom Line Investment Conference, often referred to as "TBLI". The conference organisers programme regular meetings in different regions, including Asia. Whilst in Tokyo, I stayed an additional day as I had scheduled meetings with some Japanese bankers. It was to attend one of these meetings that I exited the front door of the hotel and started to cross the stone-covered compound leading to the main road. There were tall trees in the area, all with thick trunks and heavy foliage. I heard crows screeching overhead; there were several amongst the trees. Heading for the metro station and not in any particular rush, I walked at a normal pace. At first I walked in a straight line and then I turned a corner.

The very instant I turned, I felt a feathered wing beat furiously against my hair, behind my right ear. I turned around and saw a huge black crow fluttering away. It had flapped one of its wings next to the back of my head so that it literally ruffled my hair upwards.

'You stupid bird,' I said.

The compound was spacious. There was no need to fly that close to me.

I resumed my walk towards the underground train station. Then I realised I had left some documents in the hotel room.

I retraced my steps and headed back towards the hotel. I hastened my pace. And then I yelled in pain. A rock dropped from above had hit me on the crown. I looked up and I saw a pair of large black wings, flapping, hastily flying away from me. The same idiotic bird had returned. It had dive-bombed. Attacking from above at full speed, it had struck me on the top of my head with its large beak. A few seconds previously, it had missed me because I had suddenly turned – but this time it got me. I had become an involuntary actor in a Hitchcock movie.

I swore and walked to a side-corner of the compound area. I wanted to know if the bird would attack anyone else. Was it a case of a nutty crow that attacked all passing hotel guests or was I the only one it had a grudge against? After a few minutes of watching, I gave up. It seemed the bird's animosity was only against me. I shrugged my shoulders and left the noisy area.

Three days later, I was seated comfortably on my flight back to Europe. The stewardess had served lunch and I had finished my meal. It was time for some relaxation and music. As I placed the headset over my head, I felt a sharp pain. Checking the top of my head with my fingers, I found a cherry-sized bump and crusty dried blood…

35

Malaysian Way

Kuala Terengganu, Malaysia

I was attending a WWF Malaysia trustees' board meeting in Kuala Terengganu, one of the places where the WWF Turtle Conservation team is active. What's it's goal? It's the saving of endangered turtles. With this objective in mind, various means are adopted; one method being the harvesting of turtle eggs – for safekeeping and subsequent hatching.

Another conservation activity is the buying back of eggs – a good example of the harmonisation of human needs with conservation priorities. In Terengganu, the eating of turtle eggs by the local population is a deep-rooted traditional custom. However, since turtles are an endangered species, turtle conservation work becomes a conflicting priority. As a compromise, the Terengganu State government set up a quota system. Local egg collectors are issued authorisation permits for the gathering of eggs – such eggs to be eaten by the collectors themselves or, if they prefer, sold at local markets. With the buy-back programme, numerous eggs collected are saved from the kitchen and recovered for hatching instead.

Another turtle conservation activity involves the usage of night-vision binoculars to watch over the beaches. For this task, village youths are recruited for beach patrols. Finally, there's education and training of the local population on the importance of turtle conservation.

In order that we might combine our board meeting with a direct experience of turtle conservation work in the field, the board meeting was held in Terengganu, near WWF Malaysia's Ma'Daerah turtle project.

The previous evening, at around midnight, I had witnessed baby turtles being released. I had marvelled at the sight of the tiny creatures scrambling towards the relative safety of the waiting waves. I witnessed a large leatherback turtle laying eggs. After that late night foray, the next day our board meeting commenced.

One of the trustees attending that particular board meeting was an elderly statesman. A kind person, he was respected and liked by all. He did participate and contribute, although occasionally he would make comments slightly irrelevant to the subject being debated. When I first heard him make remarks not related to the topic being discussed, I was surprised. But I kept silent, as did other board members. We would wait and then when he finished, we would resume our discussions.

It was not a big deal, to wait a few minutes for someone, especially someone we respected, to voice whatever he wanted – comments at times relevant to the subject, at other times not. It was very Malaysian, being polite and not wanting to offend anyone.

This was the unspoken and accepted procedure we had adopted.

On that particular day, one of the board members was feeling a bit brash and impatient. As the meeting progressed, the elderly statesman started to make some comments. As he did, I and the others listened politely.

All of a sudden, unexpectedly, the impatient board member spoke out.

'Now – what has that to do with the subject?' he said.

An embarrassed silence followed. The other board members and I gave the brash board member a look – a non-verbal communication to please desist from interrupting and, thankfully, he took the hint.

A brief silence followed and then we continued with our discussions as though nothing had happened. Ah, the "Malaysian Way", showing respect for the elderly…

36

Repeat Three Initials

Singapore

On my way to Malaysia, I stopped by at WWF Singapore to discuss with colleagues their progress in setting up the new offices. Furthermore, I wanted to know the results of their fundraising programmes and the general state of their finances. After we had finished discussing the various topics and were about to call it a day, Isabelle Louis brought up the subject of television interviews.

'Amy will meet you at 9.30 a.m. tomorrow to accompany you to the television studios,' said Isabelle to me. Isabelle, then head of the WWF Asia region, is Malaysian and someone who knows Singapore well – she had studied and taught there. Isabelle is of Indian origin and she was referring to Amy Tan, manager of WWF Singapore. 'Sarah, will join you there.' Amy is Singaporean and someone who diligently follows rules and regulations. Sarah, I had not yet met; she was the person who had the connection to the television studios. Isabelle had arranged a television interview for me – the goal was to raise awareness of WWF.

'I'll be there,' I said.

'I suggest you grab a taxi – and meet her at the Tanjong Pagar MRT [Mass Rapid Transit] subway exit,' said Isabelle.

'Don't forget – mention the initials "WWF" as often as you can,' Isabelle reminded me.

'I'm not sure how I can constantly repeat "WWF" without sounding silly,' I said.

Chipping in, Amy said, 'For example, you can say, "We at WWF" – or you can say, "I have worked at WWF", or "as the WWF CFO", or "in WWF's view"…'

'I see,' I said.

The next morning, I put on a dark business suit and a tie. I felt comfortable whilst I was at the hotel. However, the minute I ventured out, I found myself in an oven. Immediately, I removed my jacket but still felt hot. Singapore, after all, is located within the tropics, one degree north of the equator.

I found a cab.

Despite the open windows it was hot in the cab as it wasn't air-conditioned. Sweat trickled down my face. We headed towards the agreed meeting place.

'Sir, may I ask you – what do you do for a living?' said the driver.

'I'm in finance. One advantage is I get the privilege to dress up – to be hot and sweaty.'

The taxi driver laughed.

When we arrived, I found Amy already there. We proceeded by foot to the TV studios. There, we met Sarah. An employee from the TV company ushered the three of us into a small room next to the studio where a live broadcast was being transmitted. The live broadcast was to Asia, as we were at the studios of CNBC Asia. We did not have long to wait before another woman arrived. She introduced herself as the make-up person and she powdered my damp and shiny face. When she had finished, I had a look at the piece of paper I had brought with me – a list of the questions I would be asked.

Another TV person arrived – a man this time. He told me it was time to proceed to the next room where the broadcast was happening. 'There's a direct transmission in process – if I could ask you to be silent when we enter,' he said.

Into the room we proceeded and we stood behind the cameras. We waited for the anchor to finish her last subject.

The Asian TV presenter had an American accent. She spoke rapidly. When she ended the session she had been presenting, the commercials came on. She greeted me, we shook hands and she invited me to take the seat beside her. The commercials did not last long – and then I was on, live with her.

'And now we have someone from WWF – the World Wildlife Fund,' she announced. I could see why she had been appointed anchor. Not only was she efficient, she was also attractive and had a strong presence.

She introduced me to her audience. Then she literally bombarded me with a battery of questions – most of which had nothing to do with the list handed to me the day before. She was charming and friendly. Nevertheless I had to put myself on "full alert". Since it was live TV broadcasted for the whole of Asia I had better do a decent job in replying. She talked quickly and each time I had a fraction of a second to grasp the question. A sensible reply was called for each time but not only that, I had to somehow articulate replies that would allow me to continually slip in the initials "WWF" – my colleagues had reminded me enough times I was to do that.

And so she asked me, in her non-stop rapid-fire mode and I replied. And many a time – seven times I was later told – I repeated the initials WWF.

'We at WWF feel that…' 'Myself, as the WWF CFO…', 'I think that WWF is correct…', 'Of course that is true and that is why at WWF we…'. And so it flowed. The planned few minutes passed by and then it was all over. She thanked me warmly and I left the room.

Back at the office, my colleagues told me that the interview had gone well and that the repetition of WWF came across most naturally. The subject matter during the interview was "socially responsible investing" and in particular the investment fund that WWF had launched, the "Living Planet Fund" (now no longer linked to WWF and renamed as "One Sustainable Fund") and at the same time we wanted to get the WWF name out to the public. In that respect, both goals had been achieved.

The next day, I was scheduled to visit another TV studio, to talk to a different TV channel. This time, it was with Channel News Asia. For this second television interview, I was to meet Amy directly at the studios.

I arrived on time, as did she.

'I've never been to a TV studio before – and now it's two TV interviews in as many days,' I said.

'Well, with your practice session yesterday, you'll be able to repeat even more times the initials "WWF".'

'I'll try but there's a problem. Now that I'm used to all this TV stuff – where's my powder-woman? I can't be on TV with a shiny nose, can I?' I said, jokingly, to Amy.

'No worries,' she said.

Grinning, Amy approached me. She came near – extremely near. She opened her large handbag and took out a round metallic powder box. From it she extracted a soft pad and she powdered my face...

Hand In Honey Pot

Penang, Malaysia

I would attend WWF Malaysia board meetings approximately once each year. One year, the organisation had organised events so that a presentation for important external parties could occur immediately after the board meeting. So there I was, in a hotel's meeting room in Penang, participating in the conference when Surin Suksuwan, the then WWF Malaysia's Chief Technical Officer, approached the speaker's podium. Surin is Malay. He has short hair and, wearing a green "safari" jacket, he looked every bit the professional field conservationist.

Arriving at the platform, Surin stood confidently in front of the microphone. We listened attentively to him – "we" being WWF Malaysia trustees, some government officials and a gathering of local business leaders. I was seated in the front row.

His talk had already covered in detail environmental conservation matters relating to the nearby region of Ulu Muda, located in the state of Kedah. Surin's presentation had included statistics. He gave us information about the population of hornbills, the hectares of virgin forests already flattened, the land area still remaining, the discovery of new limestone caves and the continued existence of rare plants and exotic flowers.

Next, Surin projected a photograph onto a large screen. I saw an extremely tall tree. 'This is the Tulang tree,' he said. 'It's found in the Ulu Muda region. This tree is an exceptional tree. It grows to an immense height – about seventy metres. There's an interesting story linked to this tree. The local people are very fond of it. Do you know why?'

No one answered his rhetorical question.

'Each year, the villagers construct makeshift ladders in order to climb up these trees. Each person knows exactly which tree "belongs" to whom. There's never any trespassing. The villagers climb the trees in search of honey – this being their annual honey harvest. But they always only do this during moonless nights. As these trees are tall, each can host up to sixty – or sometimes even as many as seventy-honeycombs.

The problem, of course, is that harvesting drives the honeybees mad. To defend their hives, they will attack any intruder. The villagers, on the other hand, have no wish to be stung. Or, even worse, to fall off after being bitten – and falling would mean a seventy-metre drop…

You may ask: how do the villagers do it? Get their hands on the honey without being stung? Well, the solution is this – they only harvest during moonless nights. As each villager climbs a tree, he holds a flaming torch in hand. At first the torch provides the light for him to see where to climb. Later, the flame serves a second purpose. No, not what you think – not to burn the bees, nor to smoke the hive.

When he gets next to the hive, the villager burns some branches. Bits and pieces of the branches burst into flames. After the branches light up, hot embers start to fall to the ground. Enraged, the bees attack the embers. In the dark they only see the falling red embers. They chase and follow the "enemy", the red embers, as they fall – all of seventy metres down. By the time the bees arrive at the bottom of the jungle, the embers have burnt out. Being a moonless night, it's then pitch dark. No longer able to see, the bees cannot return to the hive. Meantime, the villager is left alone to harvest the honey…'

38

Bloodthirsty Intruders

Belum, Malaysia

Noraini Ali is the personal assistant of the WWF Malaysia Chief Executive Officer. She's Malay and she works in the Petaling Jaya office, about half an hour's drive from Kuala Lumpur, Malaysia's capital city. "Aini" as we call her, has been with WWF Malaysia for many years. One morning, she and I were on the telephone, discussing a pending trip. I was to meet with other trustees of WWF Malaysia and we would subsequently be making a trip to the rainforest, to visit a field project. This particular project was linked to WWF Malaysia's tiger conservation activities; tigers being an endangered species. There were more than a hundred thousand tigers, all countries considered, at the start of the 20th century, but today they number no more than three thousand.

'Don't forget to pack your leech socks,' Aini advised.

'What are they?' I asked.

'Well, if you wear them, the leeches – they cannot bite you.'

'They really exist, these socks? Or you're pulling my leg?'

'Believe me.'

'I can't buy such socks in Geneva. Can you get them for me?'

'Sure, I'll do that.'

A few days later, in Kuala Lumpur, I paid Aini and became the proud owner of a brand new pair of leech socks. The following day, with the socks securely packed inside my suitcase, I boarded our bus. Together with other WWF Malaysia staff we headed for Belum, a small town located within the northern part of the country near the Thai border.

We arrived at dusk. After dinner that evening, we adjourned to one of the hotel's conference rooms for a presentation by WWF Malaysia's tiger experts. We were a small group and were to be briefed on the state of tiger conservation in Malaysia. The presenters showed photographs of jungle clearings where cameras had been set up. These cameras were used to automatically take shots of passing tigers – the goal being to count the number of passing tigers within a specified geographical area. Such cameras are important as tools for tiger conservation work. They help field workers in their estimations of the evolution of tiger populations. During the presentation, what one of the speakers said surprised me.

'Recent studies included the impact of logging on the tiger population. In some locations, despite the logging, the number of tigers even increased. This could be because, due to less vegetation, the tigers can now more easily catch their prey. Or other factors could be the cause – but the truth is, right now we don't really know,' he said.

'This is most unexpected,' I said.

'Yes. We were surprised too. But we'll continue to study the matter.'

Another speaker shared with us some press clippings on the screen. One of the clippings showed three uniformed Malaysian policemen arresting a man. In the background were two white deep freezers. These were the cabinets in which the police found tiger parts.

"He doesn't know how they got there", stated the newspaper caption.

Early the next morning, I unpacked my precious leech socks. They were peculiar looking and made of plastic. They came in one standard size, available in different colours. My pair were bi-coloured – white at the top and lime green at the bottom. Not that colour matching is of any importance for walking in the jungle mud. These socks were to be worn loosely.

How did I put them on?

Firstly, I slipped on a pair of normal socks. I had a black pair on that day. Over them came the leech socks, entirely covering them. Next, I put on my walking shoes.

With my shoes on, the bottom part of the leech socks became no longer visible. The upper part (leech socks are long) of the leech socks I pulled up high and over my jeans. The result is that they effectively encircled and enclosed the lower part of my jeans. This was easily done, as there was a strong elastic band at the top end of each leech sock.

Having completed this strange dressing-up process, I became hermetically sealed from leeches. Any bloodthirsty leech searching for a good meal at my expense would have a tough time. Firstly, it would encounter resistance from my walking shoes; made of thick rubber, they would also be covered with grimy brown jungle mud. As to the mud, I guessed the leeches were used to it, so that aspect might not terribly deter any assailant. However, should a hungry leech persist and climb beyond my shoes, it would be confronted by the upper plastic portion of my leech socks. There would still be no meal possible for the raider. If it did not give up but continued further, it would next come across my thick blue jeans. Surely it could not be easy for a leech to bite through denim? All in all, I was well protected. However, having lived many years in Switzerland, I have adopted some Swiss habits, including that of trying to do things as thoroughly as possible. So out came my secret weapon.

I grabbed a red cylinder of insect repellent and I gave the whole lot – shoes, leech socks and jeans – a good and thorough spray over. Then I repeated the process.

Thus well prepared, I joined WWF Malaysia staff, along with invited guests, for our venture into the jungle. A knowledgeable local guide led us as we trekked by foot. The ground was soggy from the previous night's rainfall and the vegetation was thick. Trees and protruding bush branches were everywhere. Our guide led us through a narrow path. He slashed branches to clear the way and we made good headway into the dense jungle. We entered a clearing. The guide gave us a briefing about the special cameras attached to the tree trunks. As had been explained to us the evening before, these had been installed to capture tiger movements.

As he talked, I observed the other members of our group. Like myself, most of them had donned leech socks over their thick jeans. I looked down at my shoes – there were no leeches. Maybe that was also due to the liberal double dose of insect repellent?

Amy Tan, a colleague, was part of the group listening to our guide. Standing next to me, she had sports shoes on. The kind used for playing tennis, not jungle walking shoes.

'You're not wearing any leech socks,' I said to her.

'What are they?' she replied.

Amy was wearing a pair of white pants – city-type trousers, made of thin textile material. Coming from a city-state such as Singapore, she was probably not used to jungle walks.

Something moved on the top of her left shoe.

'Hey, Amy, there's a leech on your shoe!' an excited colleague exclaimed.

Amy immediately took a stick and brushed the leech off.

No sooner had she done that than the guide chipped in.

'There are three more clinging to your trousers,' he said.

She brushed those off.

Her not wearing leech socks had made her easy prey. The leeches seemed to know she was the most vulnerable and had concentrated their efforts on her.

'Careful – there's another one starting to climb your pants,' I said.

Amy swept that one off too.

'OK, let's go – time to move on,' said our guide.

He led us away from the clearing. In single file, our small team followed him. He took another path leading us deeper into the jungle.

After we had ventured a few paces, one of the team members, the one walking just behind Amy, spoke.

'Amy, another leech is climbing up your trousers,' he said.

Amy stopped in her tracks.

'Can I ask all of you, to please quit looking at my legs?' she said...

PART FIVE

Royalty

39

Lost In Buckingham Palace

London, England

When Prince Philip was president of WWF International, some of our meetings were held in Buckingham Palace. This would be for meetings of the WWF International board that occurred twice a year, or it could be one of the quarterly meetings of the Executive Committee. Whenever we were at the palace, the discussions would typically be held in one of the many rooms located on the ground floor. They were all impressive rooms and it was always interesting to be in them. During one such meeting, through the windows I even once saw the Queen's guards passing by on horses; another time, I saw a horse-pulled carriage rolling by.

When Prince Philip was approaching the end of his mandate as President of WWF International, I attended a final meeting at the palace. For this particular meeting with HRH, the meeting venue had changed – it was no longer the customary one-of-the-ground-floor-meeting-rooms. Instead, we convened in the library. We had never held a meeting in the library, located on the first floor of the palace. Perhaps we had been invited there because it was Prince Philip's last meeting with us. Or more likely it might have been for practical reasons – possibly because all the ground floor meeting rooms were occupied, being decorated or otherwise unavailable. Whatever the reason, that day we convened upstairs.

We were a small group as we sat around a low table located at one corner of the library, which had a vast quantity of books. They were displayed on bookshelves and stacked up high, reaching the ceiling. It was an interesting sight as I had never seen an extensive private library before, let alone one situated in a palace. Looking at all the books, I was struck by curiosity.

How did all those books get there? Did someone buy them? If so, does that mean that there is an official book-buyer? Someone appointed by Her Majesty – perhaps with a title like "Royal book purchaser for the royal household"? It's perhaps a part-time responsibility, or would it be a full-time occupation? In any case it must be a pleasant enough employment.

At the end of our meeting, I said to HRH, 'Sir, there are many books here. How does it work? I mean the process. How do all these books get here?'

HRH explained that when new books are published, the palace typically receives a copy. It was as simple as that.

That day, our meeting came to a close earlier than scheduled. During previous times, whenever discussions ended we would immediately adjourn to a dining room – if it happened to be lunchtime. Otherwise we would take our leave. That day, we did finish around lunchtime but being slightly ahead of schedule we did not straight away proceed to lunch.

'We'll meet again in fifteen minutes,' said HRH. He was always precise with his timekeeping, ensuring that all events started and, even more importantly, finished on schedule.

HRH specified where we were to re-convene. We were to walk along a certain long corridor and once we arrive at the end of it, go through the double doors.

'You'll see two pillars beside the doors – one on each side of the doors,' he said.

Our small group broke up. There were only five of us that day as it was a meeting of the Executive Committee. I left the library. I walked a bit. I took a few turnings and soon found myself alone. Not only that, I no longer knew where to go. I was lost. To complicate things, I had a sudden desperate need to find a loo. But where was I to go? Not surprisingly, there were no "this way for toilets" arrows or signboards.

I walked aimlessly. In the meantime, my discomfort grew. Then I noticed some closed doors. After an initial hesitation, I decided to try one of the doors. I opened a randomly picked door – it was someone's bedroom. I saw a small double bed but luckily no one was on it. At the far end of the room, beyond the bed, there was an open door leading to what looked like a bathroom. I took a few hesitant steps into the room. I felt uneasy as it looked like a lived-in bedroom. Whose bedroom was I in? And who on earth authorised me to enter? Not only that but with the intention to pee in someone's bathroom that's adjoining his/her bedroom in

Buckingham Palace? And what happens if, whilst I was busy, the room's occupant returned unexpectedly?

I stopped in my tracks. I turned around and quickly walked out. I closed the bedroom door. I found myself back in the corridor. But by then, Mother Nature was sending me ever more clear and strong signals. I needed to find a solution. Faced with my dilemma, I re-entered the room. This time with purpose in my stride, I rushed past the bed and I used the bathroom. Then I hurriedly left the room.

More relaxed, I was finally able to think of lunch and of finding the two pillars at the end of a corridor as mentioned by HRH. Eventually I found the corridor and, as advised, I walked towards the closed doors. Approaching the doors, I had a surprise. What I saw was the last thing I expected to find in Buckingham Palace. Flanking the double doors were two oriental pagodas, rather like Chinese-style totem poles.

I opened the double doors and I had my second surprise-when-you-open-unknown-doors-in-Buckingham Palace of the day. As the doors opened, I was confronted with a room fitted out in an extremely ornate Chinese style. The room and all furniture inside were primarily in three colours: bright red, gold or black. All the furniture had been arranged with good taste. It was possibly the style of the Ming dynasty, although I can't be sure. The whole room was not only colourful but also grandiose – I liked it.

Due to my earlier misadventure, I was therefore late. I saw that other colleagues were already there, chatting amongst themselves. Standing near the door was HRH.

'Oh, there you are,' he said as he saw me come in.

Looking at all the Chinese furniture – and being Chinese myself – I couldn't help replying, 'I feel very much at home here, sir.'

I recieved a smile back in return.

Later, as we were having our lunch, HRH explained about the Chinese furniture.

'When we got married we needed furniture. We went down to Brighton and found this lot from Queen Victoria's Pavilion…'

40

Muhammad And The Mountain

Berlin, Germany

Philippa Sekkiou was at one time my secretary. Intelligent and someone with a positive attitude, she is liked by all her colleagues. Philippa is blonde; she comes from the UK and like many British people I have met she is a fan of, and has a keen interest in, the British royal family.

When she was working for me, she would regularly come across documents to be processed or filed. At times, some of the documents had references to Prince Philip – or would require his signature. Thus, in an indirect way, she regularly had some "contact" with Prince Philip, although she had never met him.

One summer, the opportunity for Philippa to meet HRH finally arrived, due to WWF organising events in Germany. Some of the events planned included the presence of HRH. Philippa had been appointed as one of the members of the organising team. As for myself, I found it exciting that the events were to be in Berlin. It would allow me an opportunity to visit historical sites such as the Berlin Wall and the Brandenburg Gate.

And so, off to Berlin we went. On one of the evenings, the event planned was a cocktail reception for donors, to be held near Potsdamer Platz, an important square in the centre of Berlin. Our host was a notable German publishing corporation and Prince Philip was the guest of honour. The reception was to be held at the penthouse library of the company's head offices.

To attend that event, Philippa and I went together. We arrived at the building and took the lift to the penthouse floor. When our elevator stopped and the twin doors slid open, we found ourselves in a large and crowded reception room. There were many guests, most with drinks in hand and they were talking amongst themselves and forming constantly changing groups.

'Gosh! At last, my chance to meet Prince Philip,' said Philippa.

'At receptions, he often walks around, mingling with different groups,' I said.

'I can't wait to tell my family I have met Prince Philip.'

'Let's see where he is,' I said.

'What should I do?' she said.

'When you see him just place yourself in his way. This way, your turn will automatically come.'

I surveyed the room and I located Prince Philip. I pointed out to Philippa as to where he was. Following my advice, she left me. She went and placed herself along the path of his expected route. Philippa waited patiently whilst HRH talked with a small group. He left the group. She saw him approaching. However, at the last second, he turned left and was moving away. Unexpectedly, he had changed his "flight path".

HRH greeted another group. Not easily daunted, Philippa again placed herself in the way of HRH's newly chosen direction. She saw Prince Philip getting nearer. As he took leave of this group, he advanced a few more steps towards her. Alas, at the last moment, once more, just before Philippa's "turn" came, Prince Philip changed course. He ended up talking with someone else. Being a determined young lady, Philippa tried yet again. She waited and, unbelievably, just when she was ready to say hello to HRH, he again changed direction.

'It's so frustrating,' she said to me.

'Oh?'

'It's as though he doesn't want to meet me. Maybe I shouldn't have put myself in his path – by now I would have met him.'

'You missed him three times?'

'Yes, each time he turned at the last instant.'

The evening had run on. The reception would not last the whole night. I had to quickly find a solution. For my secretary it was important that she meet HRH and so it became a priority for me.

'I've an idea,' I said.

'Which is?'

'Just wait here.'

'What's your solution?'

'Leave it to me – but please don't move. Stay here.'

'OK,' she said.

I negotiated my way through the noisy drinking crowd. I found Prince Philip somewhere in the middle of the room. I approached him when he was just about to join another group of invitees. Due to my interception, this group must have felt like Philippa did – that they "missed their turn".

I greeted Prince Philip.

'Sir, if I may make a request. My secretary – she's here this evening. She's British and she would be most thrilled to meet you.'

'Sure.' Then, most unexpectedly, he added, 'I'll come – where is she?'

'I'll bring her to you, sir. It's Muhammad who has to come to the Mountain…'

41

Mother Hen

London, England

Before I joined WWF International, I decided I would do some research. As I did, I learnt that the board of trustees included HRH Prince Philip. He was president of the organisation.

'Good of him to lend his name to the cause,' I said to a friend.

When I eventually started working at WWF, I was much surprised. Prince Philip was not "just lending" his name. He indeed had a genuine and keen interest in conservation. In fact he devoted a significant amount of time and energy on environmental matters.

HRH attended our meetings, he read bulky documentation and fully participated in all important decisions. His level of personal involvement was considerable. I was also many a time impressed by how patient he remained, even during the periods when some WWF colleagues behaved in a trying manner.

'He really is interested? Does he invest the necessary time?' as a new employee, I had asked a colleague.

'Yes, he's someone committed to our cause. And you know, we sometimes even have meetings in Buckingham Palace.'

'Is that true?' I asked.

A couple of months later, as I left the Regent's Park Hilton and walked onto the hotel's exterior compound, I saw three black cabs. They were waiting in line just across the courtyard. I raised a hand to signal that I needed a taxi and, instantly, the driver of the first cab drove over to me.

He slid down his vehicle's window.

'Where to, sir?' he said.

'Buckingham Palace, please,' I said.

'Where to, sir?' he repeated, raising the pitch of his voice.

'Buckingham Palace,' I repeated.

The man gave me an indulgent smile.

'You mean Buckingham Palace *ROAD* sir?'

'No, I mean Buckingham Palace.'

After our brief exchange, I entered the cab and we headed off. The traffic flow was smooth. Passing Baker Street, our car went down Oxford Street and soon we were cruising along Park Lane. Approaching the rear of the palace grounds at Hyde Park Corner, the traffic became congested and our progress slowed to a snail's pace. The cabbie drove onto Constitution Hill, one of the roads that led to the palace.

'You've a meeting with Her?' he said.

Which "Her" was he referring to? Did he mean the Queen? After all, this was her home we were heading to. Or did he mean Princess Diana – The Princess Diana? Diana was alive in those days and was often featured in the British media. Surely he meant the Queen since Diana's home was in Kensington Palace?

'Which "Her" are you referring to?' I said.

'Princess Diana of course – she's very attractive, our Princess of Wales. Are you seeing her – or has the Queen invited you?'

'Well, neither.'

'But you're going to Buckingham Palace?'

'Yes.'

As he spoke, our taxi arrived at the palace. The cabbie drove his car towards the front of the gates located to the right side (right side when facing the building) of the palace.

'What do we do now? Do I drop you off here? Or do we try to go in?' he said.

'Go on in.'

The car pulled up at the gates and stopped.

'Good morning, sir,' said the guard.

'May I have your name, please?' he said.

I gave my name. He consulted his list. This took no time at all. There were only a few names on it.

'Yes, you're expected.'

Thus authorised, we drove onto the palace compound where, with a cheerful goodbye greeting, the driver dropped me off. Leaving him, I found myself, for the first time, within the grounds of Buckingham

Palace- the Buckingham Palace that I had many a time viewed on television and seen photographs of in various newspapers and glossy magazines. With one arm clutching my briefcase and much curiosity combined with excited anticipation, I proceeded towards the right wing of the palace.

That was the first of a few trips I made to the palace. Each time I found it interesting, probably because it's so different from normal everyday life. For a typical meeting, I would arrive at the right wing where a small reception area is located. This area has a tiny window and looking out through it there is no view – except for a few parked cars. There I would wait until others also expected to attend the scheduled meeting arrived. The size of our group varied, typically between four and ten – depending on the nature of the meeting and the subjects to be discussed. Once all expected attendees had gathered, Brigadier Miles Hunt-Davis, Prince Philip's secretary, would escort us to that day's meeting venue.

Miles' full name, complete with title, is Brigadier Sir Miles Hunt-Davis. I can best describe Miles by quoting the *Daily Telegraph*, which in December 2007 wrote the following:

"With his white hair, clipped voice and taste for elephant polo, Brigadier Sir Miles Hunt-Davis is every inch the swashbuckling military man. Since retiring from the services in 1991, he has built a successful second career to become arguably the third most important civilian in the Royal Household as the private secretary to the Duke of Edinburgh."

Typically, Miles would lead the way. There are countless corridors within the palace. When I walked along these corridors some doors I passed would be ajar, revealing offices. Offices such as these could exist anywhere in London, but these were different – they were located within Buckingham Palace.

As we progressed through the corridors, once in a while we would reach an intersection, whereby our corridor would cross a passageway. Whenever we approached any such intersection, Miles would instantly pause. He would extend both arms outwards with his palms facing backwards, i.e. towards us. This way, with his special traffic-cop gesture, akin to a mother hen stretching out her wings to stop her chicks, he would time and again stop us neatly in our tracks. I thought nothing of his gesture. When he walked, I walked. When he extended his arm and stopped, I stopped, as did all others. One day, it dawned on me that his was a peculiar gesture.

'Why do you, at each intersection, extend both arms to stop us?' I asked Miles.

'Just in case She's passing,' said Miles.

But I never saw Her, not even once...

Playing Truant

Vienna, Austria

Our conference in Vienna had been planned to run over a few days. On day three, towards the end of a long afternoon, it was starting to become tedious. Some of the speakers were repeating themselves and I felt a need for some outside air. I looked around the conference room to see who was sitting nearby.

I saw Miles was just behind me. 'Miles, do you find, too, that this is getting a bit long? Shall we go for a walk?' I whispered to him.

'Good idea.'

We discreetly slipped out of the conference room, skipping whatever remained of the last session of that afternoon.

A short taxi ride and we reached the town centre. Leaving the cab, we were not sure where to go. Neither of us had visited Vienna before – and in those days smart phones did not exist.

'Now where shall we go?' I asked.

That was when I saw yet another advantage of having HRH as WWF's President.

'I'll call the Queen's Secretary,' said Miles.

After the phone call, Miles and I decided to walk to Hotel Sacher for tea and cakes. On our way, we bumped into Babar Ali. Babar was the then WWF International Treasurer and one of my bosses. He was with Altaf Saleem.

'What are you two doing here?' said Babar.

'Same as you two,' I replied…

Royal President's Remarks

London, England

During my years at WWF, I met HRH Prince Philip quite a number of times. This could be at meetings that he presided over or it could be during fundraising functions. Having seen him in action running various meetings, I have much respect for him. Many a time I observed how he remained patient, even when handling those meeting participants who had decided to behave in a tiresome manner – by no means a rare event. During meetings, HRH was meticulous with timekeeping, constantly ensuring that participants kept to the point. Often he had interesting and pertinent comments to make said at the right time and with the precise and appropriate choice of words. Some examples of relevant remarks by HRH Prince Philip follow:

London, England   Ghost Door

I was in a small conference room in Buckingham Palace, together with Prince Philip and five others. We were having discussions. The door leading into the room was closed. Then, slowly, the door moved slightly ajar. The door stopped moving. I looked at it. No one came in. The door closed. A second later the door moved again. It opened ever so slightly. Again it stopped moving. No one came in. The door closed.

Two seconds later, the door moved again. It opened slowly.

'Either you come in or you don't. Why don't you make up your mind,' Prince Philip said.

The door closed and that was the last I heard of it…

Montreux, Switzerland   Long-Winded

Someone was making a presentation and he kept on talking, repeating what he had already said. Together with colleagues, I endured the speaker's long-windedness.

'Why don't you stop farting all over the place and get to the point?' Prince Philip said.

The presentation ended soon after…

London, England   No Fun To Be A Royal

We were in an office in Buckingham Palace. Prince Philip was looking at some newspapers that laid flat on his desk – this was just before our meeting was to commence. He was reading some negative press comments about some trees in Windsor that had been cut down.

'I can't even chop down a few trees in my own garden,' he said.

London, England   Chinese Veggies

As we were finishing lunch in Buckingham Palace, Prince Philip related to us an incident. It happened when he was travelling in China.

'During my trip, I was taken to visit many interesting places. I followed my hosts everywhere. They were courteous and attentive. One morning, after a few visits, we arrived at a vegetable market. By this time, I needed to relieve myself. I told my hosts I needed a pee.'

'"Yes, sir. Of course, sir," they replied. I waited but nothing happened. No one told me where I was to go – but what puzzled me was the agitation. My hosts then engaged in animated discussions. I couldn't figure out what all the fuss was about. Surely people in China need to pee too. After what seemed an eternity, an apologetic official came up to me. "Sorry, sir, so sorry sir, out of season, sir…" he said.'

44

Prince Albert's Authorisation

Monaco

In 1954, Princess Grace of Monaco created an annual event: the Rose Ball. This prestigious event is held during March each year in Monaco in aid of the Princess Grace Foundation. Observing the success of this ball, Mario Fetz, the then head of the fundraising department, decided WWF would hold a similar annual event. Mario is Swiss and he originates from the Italian part of Switzerland. Of all the directors of fundraising I have worked with at WWF, I consider Mario the one who was the most able. He's someone who is optimistic and always ready for a new challenge. With Mario's initiative, the concept of the WWF Panda Ball was born.

The aim of the event was to achieve multiple fundraising goals. Firstly, to maintain relationships with existing donors, as out of sight often meant out of mind. Periodic contact with donors was desirable. Another ambition was to reach out to and attract, new supporters.

The first-ever WWF Panda Ball, attended by over two hundred guests, was held in Lausanne, Switzerland. Over the years, WWF's reputation as organiser of a well-run annual gala event for a good cause increased.

After a successful launch in Lausanne, the venue of the ball was later shifted to a quiet town along the shores of Lake Geneva. It was held at The Montreux Palace – since renamed Fairmont Montreux, a member of the Leading Hotels Of The World. Each year, there would be a different guest of honour. Once it was Prince Philip, at another time it was Prince Albert of Monaco and another year the expected guest of honour was Queen Noor of Jordan, although in this particular case she had to cancel at the last moment due to unexpected circumstances that rendered her visit impossible.

After many years of holding the event in Switzerland, it was decided that the location would be shifted, on a one-off basis, to Monte Carlo.

Prince Albert had invited WWF to host the ball in his Principality and WWF had accepted. It was considered that having the event in Monaco would increase awareness of WWF and its conservation work in the Principality. This would surely be beneficial in terms of fundraising goals. We all knew that in terms of density of rich people per square kilometre, there are not many places on earth that would be able to outdo Monaco.

The ball was held, one spring evening, in Monaco. The venue chosen was "Le Sporting" in Monaco – a location often used for important functions. The place is renowned for the way the roof was built. On a clear evening the rooftop can open up to reveal the night sky and its glittering stars.

When the appointed evening came, guests arrived at Le Sporting.

'Looks like a Hollywood Oscar awards evening,' a donor said to me.

The majority of the men were wearing black bow ties. The women wore glamorous long dresses, had elaborate hair-dos and many were wearing expensive jewellery.

Two reception areas for cocktails had been organised. There was the main reception area for guests and, in addition, a smaller reception area had been set up to provide the more important donors with an opportunity to personally meet with Prince Albert.

I helped direct the VIP guests to this special area. In total there were about thirty men and women VIPs. Some of them had given substantial donations in the past.

When we arrived in the designated reception area, I chatted with the guests. The various invitees mingled with each other and we sipped cocktails. One end of the reception area opened onto a large outdoor terrace that had commanding scenic views of Monaco and the blue Mediterranean Sea. Some of the guests spilled over onto this terrace. It was a warm evening and I joined them. Conversations covered Monaco, the venue of the ball and WWF's conservation work. When the guests had been circulating for approximately fifteen minutes, Prince Albert arrived. He walked in accompanied by a tall attractive blonde – this was Miss Charlene Wittstock.

At that time, Prince Albert and Charlene were not yet married – but, in her long white evening gown, Charlene already looked every part a princess. As she walked into the room, I saw, sewn onto the bottom part of her gown, a huge black and white image of a Panda. That dress was an immediate smash hit. It made headlines in newspapers and magazines in a number of countries, especially in Spain, because for this particular event there happened to be a large number of Spanish guests and media attending – these being pre-Spanish financial and property crisis days.

Charlene indeed looked stunning. Later, during the evening, whilst my wife and I were chatting with her, I found that not only was she good-looking, she was also a fun and witty person.

'She's charming,' said Françoise. 'She's not stuffy – and I like her jokes.'

Following the reception, all guests proceeded to the main hall. During dinner, an auction was held. The auction items included an outrageous looking and ostentatious men's belt. It was chunky, large, metallic and, in fact, downright ugly.

'I think even Elvis would blush if asked to wear it,' I said to the person sitting next to me. Following the auction there were the usual speeches and expressions of appreciation – as customary at gala dinners.

When we had finished dinner and coffee had been served, the music started. I found it too loud. Some of the guests proceeded onto the dance floor and started to dance. Towards the end of the evening, as Françoise danced, she saw that Prince Albert and Charlene were sitting at the head table, not far from her. Whilst she was dancing, Prince Albert and Charlene decided it was time for them to leave. As Charlene was about to go, she went up to Françoise to bid her farewell. She kissed Françoise on both cheeks (they had a few laughs together earlier on) – a gesture often done in France. Françoise was pleasantly surprised. She had met Charlene only just that evening at the VIP reception and found that it was a friendly gesture on Charlene's part.

Spontaneously, turning to Prince Albert, she said, 'She's charming – you *must* marry her!'

'That's a kind comment,' said Prince Albert.

'And thank you for the permission,' added Prince Albert…

45

Only Sara Dares

Seville, Spain.

Shortly after WWF was founded in 1961, the organisation worked with the Spanish Government to purchase a section of the Guadalquivir delta marshes in Andalucia, southern Spain. Thus was established the Coto Donana National Park. This was and remains, an important wetlands area. It's of significant importance as it's a stopping point for migratory birds, as well as one of the last refuges of the Spanish imperial eagle and the Iberian lynx. To celebrate its fortieth anniversary, WWF decided to host a series of events in Seville, near WWF's first major project, the Coto Donana.

For the anniversary dinner, I was assigned the task of picking up by taxi the Honourable Sara Morrison, who was the then WWF International President. Claude Martin the Director General would normally have been the person who would have escorted Sara – but on that particular day he had other VIPs to look after. He had to "worry'" not only about Prince Philip but also Prince Bernhard of the Netherlands.

At the appointed time I hailed a taxi and headed for Sara's hotel. Upon arrival, I found her standing by the hotel's entrance. She entered the taxi and we exchanged greetings. As the car drove away, she voiced her thoughts about the speech she would be making that evening.

The cab took us to a stately-looking building set within extensive lush gardens. This was where the dinner and the WWF "birthday" celebrations were to be held. We entered the gardens. Sara and I marvelled at the welcoming committee, young women gaily dressed in colourful Andalusian costumes, flanking both sides of the pathway. They were elegant, with their short jackets and flat black hats typical of the region. As we walked through the compound, we were greeted with smiles and the lively music of strumming Spanish guitars.

Upon arrival, at the entrance of the building, we saw Claude Martin was already there.

'Oh, there you both are – but you took the wrong entrance. You should've arrived at the other side – that's the official entrance,' he said.

'Don't be silly,' replied Sara. 'How on earth are we to know the official entrance is on the other side? Where the cabby dropped us there was music and a welcoming committee – so it must've been the right entrance. Anyway, what's important is that we're here.'

Claude laughed.

He looked at Sara. Then he turned to face me.

'You know that Sara and Prince Philip are good friends?' he said.

'That I know,' I said.

'They get on extremely well together. They often share laughs. And you will *never* guess how she can joke with HRH in a way no one on this planet will ever dare to.'

'And how's that?' I said.

Claude gently brought the flat of his hand to the top of Sara's head.

'By jokingly touching Prince Philip on the head,' he said…

Danish Way

Nyon, Switzerland

Johan Schroeder was at one time President of WWF Denmark. He and I were having a drink at the bar of the hotel La Barcarolle in Nyon. We were comparing the relative success of fundraising in different countries. In particular, we discussed the 1001 programme.

As the members comprised of individuals, over time some of the members would pass away and thus replacements would need to be found. I knew some countries were better at recruitment than others.

'It's interesting: the Danish case,' I said.

'What do you mean?' Johan said.

'For a small country, you've been recruiting many new members. A lot, in terms of the relative size of Denmark.'

'I know,' he said.

'How do you do it? What's the secret?'

'You know, in Denmark, like in a few European countries, we too have our royal family supporting us.'

'How's that different from other countries, where they also have royals?'

'Do you know what I say to all our potential 1001 members?'

'No.'

'Oh, so you would like to meet the Prince Consort over dinner? No problem – of course I can arrange that,' he said.

'Up to now, nothing unusual,' I said.

'Ah, but I tell them, please pay up first…'

Rascal

Gstaad, Switzerland

'Is Prince Philip still involved with WWF?' John Nash asked me as the coffee arrived. We had just finished an excellent three-course dinner. We were in a restaurant that was tastefully decorated in the style of an elegant mountain chalet. This was in Gstaad, a fashionable Swiss mountain resort. It was by then early morning, close to 1 a.m., but we were alert, enjoying the HSBC-sponsored dinner.

John's an Englishman and he knows Prince Philip well. When I first started working at WWF, John was the treasurer. We were often at meetings together, including on occasion with HRH – and time and again I had the opportunity to observe John's abilities. I have much respect for him. He is the image of the British gentleman. He's also astute and intelligent. John lives in the Gstaad area, in a house where access is solely via its own exclusive cable car. I have never been to his place but was told that at the site where one boards the cable car, there is a sign that asks potential visitors a question.

"Do you really have to come?" is what's written on the board.

I replied to John.

'Yes, Prince Philip is still involved,' I said.

'You know, he's such a kind and thoughtful man,' John said. 'I've seen many examples of that.'

'I know, I've seen that too,' I said.

'You know what happened recently?' John asked.

'No, tell me.'

'One of my nephews, he's a student at Eton College.'

'One of your British schools – near Windsor.'

'That's the one. Well, my nephew asked if there was any chance he could meet Prince Philip during one of his Windsor Castle stays. He told me he would be thoroughly thrilled – so I asked HRH if he could meet my nephew.'

'And?'

'He agreed. My nephew was received at Windsor Castle. Prince Philip was kind and thoughtful. He asked my nephew about his studies, his hobbies, his ambitions and generally tried his best to make the young man feel at ease.'

'Nice of him,' I said.

John seemed pleased.

'And do you know what he said to my nephew?'

'No, what did he say?'

'Now tell me – how is he, your rascal of an uncle?'

48

Her Serene Highness

Zurich, Switzerland

Attending the 50th anniversary celebrations of WWF, held in a large conference hall in Zurich, I took my seat for the dinner. I sat next to Tatiana Gortchacow. Tatiana's Russian and she has a title; her title is Princess, which makes her Princess Tatiana. I had met her when she used to work for the fundraising department at WWF.

'How nice to see you again,' I said.

'I'm glad to see you too.'

'In fact, we've never sat next to each other at any official dinner function,' I said.

'You're right. Anyway, now that I've left [WWF] I hardly attend any WWF events. But my daughter recently attended a function.'

'I don't think I've ever met her.'

'She's attractive, my daughter. You'd enjoy her company.'

'I'm sure.'

'But she's happily married, I must add,' she said.

'By the way, since you are sitting next to me, it's just the opportunity for me to ask you…' I said.

'About?'

'Yourself and your title – you never told me about it.'

'Sure. What would you like to know?'

'Your parents – they came from Russia? How did your title come about?'

'Yes, my parents came to Switzerland from Russia. But you know, we are not "royals",' she said.

'"Royals"? Versus what – what's the difference?' I said.

'Well, "royals" are always linked to a monarchy.'

'I see.'

'When there's a monarch, the title-holders are then "royals".'

'Like the Romanovs?' I said.

'Yes, they were "royals". We're not – but our lineage is old. Since 1400, so before them.'

'"Royals" or "non-royals", what difference does it make in everyday life?'

'The only difference is in how we address someone. "Your Royal Highness" is the form used for "royals".'

'And for "non-royals"?'

'"Your Serene Highness".'

'I see. Now I understand why we address Prince Albert as "Your Serene Highness".'

'You got it.'

'So I should address you as "Your Serene Highness"?'

'True,' replied Tatiana with a laugh.

Tatiana's a tall woman. She can get quite emotional and expressive at times. She did her job of fundraising well when she was with WWF – including on occasion dealing with difficult colleagues or over-demanding donors. Whilst on most days she would have everything under control, there have been occasions when she would be really exasperated.

'You remember Joel, the concierge at WWF?' she said.

'Yes.'

'And Dorothy Bray from the human resources department?'

'Yes, of course,' I said.

'Well, one day the concierge had asked me about my title, just like you're doing now.'

'So?'

'I explained to him all this "royals" and "non-royals" stuff. And I had just finished explaining that "Your Serene Highness" was the formal way to address me – when Dorothy, who, having overheard us, chipped in:

'"I can tell you, on some days she's certainly not serene at all!" she said...

49

King Of Tonga

Nyon, Switzerland

It was evening. I was sitting with some colleagues in a small Swiss restaurant. They had come from different countries where WWF had offices. We had just finished dinner, which consisted of Swiss fondue (a cheese and wine mix, into which are dipped small pieces of bread) and were chatting amongst ourselves, when Claude Martin stood up. He welcomed us and mentioned that he hoped we were enjoying the evening.

'And now, friends and colleagues,' he said, 'I shall tell you about the King of Tonga.'

'Oh no, not the King of Tonga again,' said a colleague.

'Yes,' said Claude.

'What's this all about?' a relatively new employee asked.

He was considered new as he had been with us less than three years, whereas most in the room had been working at WWF for at least five years.

'I'll tell you – it's about the King of Tonga,' said Claude.

'Is Tonga in Africa?' my neighbour asked me quietly.

'No – it's in the Pacific Ocean,' I said.

'Sounds interesting.'

'It is – if it's the first time you hear the story,' I said.

'And now, about the King of Tonga…' Claude announced. 'The King of Tonga once made a state visit to Great Britain. The King's a big man. He's also someone who enjoys pomp and tradition. Respecting the King's importance and his wishes, the palace had scheduled a formal welcoming ceremony. When the day of his visit arrived, the Queen set forth to meet him. She rode in a gilded open carriage, pulled by four magnificent brown horses. The whole scene was colourful and splendid – exactly how the King would have liked it.

When the King disembarked from his plane, the Queen greeted him.

Together, they proceeded to the carriage. She ascended the vehicle and he followed her. They took their seats, with the King sitting next to the Queen – both facing the horses. The liveryman gave a command and the carriage made its way to Buckingham Palace. It was most ceremonial and the King enjoyed it.

But, as the horses trotted along, a problem arose. Earlier that day, one of them had eaten far too much hay. Due to indigestion, plus the strain of pulling the heavy carriage, it started to emit certain foul smells. The King was immediately aware but, being polite, he said nothing. The Queen, too had noted what had happened but made no comment.

'The carriage continued its journey. Arriving in London, it travelled along the main roads. Then it turned off to pass through some cobblestone-paved streets, which somewhat jostled the carriage. Well-wishers standing alongside the pavements waved. The Queen waved back. Throughout the journey whenever the same horse emitted unpleasant gases, the King endured in silence. As for the Queen, she continued to make polite conversation – pretending to be unaware of the smells.

Finally, to everyone's relief, the carriage pulled up in front of Buckingham Palace. As the vehicle came to a halt, the stench became overpowering. At this stage the Queen felt she ought to say something.

"Your Highness, please do excuse me for that smell," she said.

"Oh, I thought it was the horses but don't worry about it," replied the King.'

50

Tiny Scrap Of Paper

Buenos Aires, Argentina

The location of our meetings with Prince Philip varied. Sometimes we met at WWF offices, sometimes at Buckingham Palace and at times at locations where other conferences had already been scheduled. We even once had a meeting at Heathrow Airport, in a special area, in a place only VVIPs could use, I was told. One summer our meeting was scheduled at Windsor Castle as Prince Philip was residing there at that time.

Arriving at Windsor Castle, we had been shown into the waiting room by one of the secretaries. As we waited, I looked out through the windows, admiring the views of the impeccably kept garden grounds. The room itself, especially the walls, caught my attention.

Throughout the room there were large wooden panels covering all the walls. These panels were not the kind of elegant panelling typically found in smart corporate boardrooms or possibly in posh clubs or hotel libraries. These panels had a rough look. They consisted of wide wooden beams stacked vertically along the walls. They were of the kind you would expect to find on ceilings of farmhouses or in olden days' sailing ships. But these beams were not on the ceilings – they covered the walls. They were neatly aligned, vertically. They looked extremely old and I saw there were multiple small holes in each beam. No doubt the work of insects.

As I stared at the beams on the wall, I noticed next to the door, stuck on the wall, a small metallic plate. There was an inscription on it. The inscription informed that each and every beam had been dismantled from a dungeon and transferred, piece by single piece, to Windsor Castle.

'If we're in such a waiting room – maybe it's a bad sign,' a colleague said.

'Perhaps,' I replied.

After a short wait we were escorted to a conference room for our meeting. Luckily, even though we started the day waiting in the "dungeon waiting room", our meeting that day began and ended, on a normal note, with no hitches. When the meeting ended, we proceeded to cross the internal private garden area at Windsor Castle, heading towards an exit at the far end. As we walked, I looked around and I admired the splendour of the castle. Everything looked just perfect. Originally built by William the Conqueror in the 11th century, the castle has a medieval look.

'I can easily imagine armoured knights on horseback riding around here,' I said to a colleague as we walked.

It was very quiet. I looked at the high walls and as I was looking at the multitude of windows overlooking the gardens, a colleague turned to me.

'There mustn't be much activity here during summer. That being the case, maybe She's observing us through one of those windows, crossing Her interior gardens,' he said.

Years later, I was in South America - Buenos Aires to be precise - having lunch with a group of colleagues. We were in one of the larger conference rooms of the Park Hyatt Buenos Aires. For this particular meal, HRH Prince Philip sat at our table; an event that does not often occur. Typically, whenever there is an official event, the head table, where HRH would sit, would be reserved for VVIPs or VIPs. These could be key government officials, other royalty or major donors – but that day WWF was not hosting any official external event. It was a lunch break during some internal workshops. About ten of us sat around a large circular table.

As was usual, whenever HRH spoke, we would all listen attentively. He was telling us something or other. As he was speaking, I saw Miles walk up to him. Approaching HRH to his right, he leaned over and whispered in Prince Philip's ear. He then handed him a tiny piece of folded paper. HRH unfolded the paper.

'Oh, Windsor's burning,' he said.

HRH then slid the note into the breast pocket of his jacket and he continued with whatever he had been saying before the interruption.

At that moment, the whole incident made no particular impression on me. That same evening, however, when I was back at my hotel room and had switched on the television set, I found, on every channel, vivid images of Windsor Castle in flames. Recalling HRH's lunchtime reading of the note, it struck me that I had witnessed a prime example of the British "stiff upper lip" in action…

51

What One Greek Said

Bakthapur, Nepal

Royalty has always played an important role at WWF. This has been the case right from the beginning. When WWF was first founded in 1961, Prince Philip was invited to be the president. However, he had declined as he had already accepted other not-for-profit appointments. As an alternative, he had recommended his friend Prince Bernhard of the Netherlands, who kindly accepted. However, in later years, as soon as his diary allowed him the possibility to devote time to WWF, Prince Philip did assume the position of President of WWF International. That was in 1981. He remained president for many years, until 1996. Today, as President Emeritus, he is still involved with WWF, although to a lesser degree.

Having royalty involved at WWF means that the royal connection will attract more donors and supporters; people who otherwise might not be as interested in WWF's conservation and/or fundraising activities. This was the situation, especially during the early years, when royalty lent increased credibility to the newly founded organisation. Last but certainly not least, royalty substantially extends WWF's reach and influence. For example, if a letter sent to a president of any country had been signed by Prince Philip, we were quite certain that the letter will receive appropriate attention. Many different royalties were and are, involved with WWF. In addition to Prince Philip and Prince Bernhard, there are others – the King of Spain, the King of Sweden, some Malaysian sultans, the Prince Consort of Denmark, Queen Noor of Jordan and Prince Albert II of Monaco, to name but a few. Typically, the role of royalty is to help push the cause for the WWF organisation in the country where the royalty resides. As an example, the King of Sweden is more involved in the activities of WWF Sweden, although he might also participate in events organised by WWF International.

Some members of royalty contribute substantial time to WWF International's activities whilst still remaining strongly associated with WWF in the country where they live. One such person is Prince Philip, the Duke of Edinburgh. As president, he presided over meetings of the board of WWF International, on average four times a year. In addition there were the quarterly executive committee meetings, followed by a yearly event, the WWF Annual Conference. There were fundraising events, where the Duke's presence always added prestige, thereby improving attendance and fundraising results. There were also other events where Prince Philip again devoted time, such as the Duke of Edinburgh Conservation Award – or there may be invitations for cocktails with Prince Philip at Buckingham Palace in appreciation of donors who have contributed substantial sums.

The year we were in Kathmandu for the annual conference, Prince Philip was the then President of WWF International. I was there attending the WWF Annual Conference. In addition to attending the conference, I had presentations to make at the board and the executive committee meetings of WWF International – plus I had to advise some WWF country managers on financial matters.

It was there that one colleague broke the news to me.

'The Pope – he arrived too early,' he said.

'So what did you do?' I asked.

'We didn't know what to do with him. Someone pointed to a plastic chair and suggested he took a seat in the meantime.'

'He couldn't have been pleased,' I said.

'No, he wasn't.'

Located within the Kathmandu Valley in Nepal, Bakthapur is a well-known historical town. It has a medieval look, many old buildings, huge public squares, pagodas, ancient temples and palaces. A UNESCO World Heritage site, it had been the capital of Nepal during the 15th century. It was here, in Bakthapur, that the Pope arrived.

WWF had planned a series of conferences and functions in Nepal. These events had been planned during the same time period that the Maoist rebels in Kathmandu had been extremely active. Initially, we had concluded we would not be holding any conferences in Nepal because of the unrest. However, through intermediaries, the Maoists had been sounded out. They were asked whether there would be a quiet period if we came. They had considered the pros and cons of WWF holding a conference in Kathmandu and had decided we could be classified as "good guys"'. That being the case, they would cool things down during the week when we would be there. They promised to not disturb the peace during the entire duration of our visit. As such they would undertake no new activities. Pursuits that otherwise might have covered mundane subjects such as bombing yet another factory building…

Assured with such good news we were able to progress with the programme for events in Nepal. The plan was to stagger ceremonies in order of importance, culminating with a grand finale on the last day. Throughout the week there would be an important central theme: the coming together of all of the world's main religions for one united cause – that of environmental conservation. Together with ARC, the Alliance of Religions and Conservation, WWF had planned many events. Most of these would be held in Kathmandu, with the grand finale to occur at Bakthapur. It was to attend this final ceremony, which had been planned for the last day, that the Pope had arrived.

The week had started well, with a most original opening ceremony. A Jain priest had travelled from India to join us. Being a true Jain, whenever he walked he did so holding a broom in front of him, continually sweeping the ground so as not to inadvertently step on any of God's living creatures, in particular the smaller ones.

Attending the opening ceremony were Christians, Buddhists, Muslims, Hindus, Jews, Jains and Parsis. To kick off the event, all the attendees joined a procession, with the Jain priest leading. The priest walked slowly. We, too walked, in similarly measured steps, whilst all the time maintaining a respectful silence. It was not a long walk and we covered only a short distance. Starting from the manicured gardens of the Holiday Inn Kathmandu, we headed for the hotel's main conference room.

For the procession, Prince Philip walked directly behind the priest. Following him were invited dignitaries, including local politicians as well as major donors. Bringing up the rear was everyone else, including myself. As he walked, the priest continued to sweep the ground unfailingly in front of him. Each sweep of the broom to the right, always followed by a careful brush to the left.

'The hotel staff – they'll have less floor cleaning tonight,' a colleague whispered to me.

A few minutes later, we arrived at the meeting area and the conference commenced. No sooner had we started than the Jain left us, embarking on his solitary return journey – sweeping as he went.

Following the first day's ceremony, various activities were held during the week. Then came Friday, the day planned for the last main event. Multiple arrangements had been made. Banner-waving schoolchildren would line the streets and multi-coloured flags would be erected on high poles to flutter in the wind. Furthermore, it was arranged for music to be audible everywhere. Drums, trumpets and cymbals would be omnipresent and the hundreds of participants would arrive, coming in from different directions, to converge as one big mass of humanity at the town's main square. At the square there would be yet more banners and even more loud music waiting to welcome the participants. For this final day's closing ceremony every major religion of the world would be represented.

It was during the hectic preparation period prior to the event itself that the Pope had arrived. My colleagues had referred to him as the "Pope", but in fact his proper title is "Patriarch" – head of the Greek Orthodox Church, therefore someone of great importance. The Greek Orthodox Church is the main Christian Church in the Middle East and Eastern Europe. Sometimes referred to as the Orthodox Church or the Eastern Church, this church is estimated to have in excess of one hundred million followers.

The Patriarch had flown in from New York. Due to limited airline flight schedules, he had arrived early, at around four in the afternoon. Consequently, there was no formal reception committee to meet and greet him. The WWF staff members he had come across were not accustomed to protocol and thus did not know how to handle the situation. Unable to find a solution, someone had hesitantly suggested the Patriarch should wait until the evening's sessions commenced. And that had apparently (as I was told) resulted in one not too happy Patriarch.

'How're you going to handle this?' I asked.

'We'll tell Claude when he arrives. He'll know what to do.'

Claude Martin was the then Director General of WWF International. 'I'm but a Swiss peasant,' he would often say, but most of us would not take him seriously when he said that – and the few who did would quickly realise they had made a mistake. Knowing Claude, we all felt confident he would find a way to defuse the situation.

As evening approached, the ceremonies commenced and huge crowds filled the square. Chairs had been put in place – hundreds of them. These chairs were quickly occupied. Standing behind the rows of chairs were huge crowds, comprising locals and foreigners. Amidst this multitude of noisy and excited people, right in the middle of the public square, a large wooden podium had been erected. On this elevated podium there were two armchairs but what stood out was the single two-seater sofa placed in the centre of the stage. It looked most comfortable. Seated very upright on this sofa were to be found two occupants: one was Prince Philip – the other was Claude.

I saw a colleague ascend the steps of the podium. He went to Claude and whispered in his ear. Claude spoke to Prince Philip, who nodded. Claude left the podium and went straight to the Patriarch. He greeted the Patriarch warmly and offered his apologies (I was told). Next, Claude escorted the Patriarch towards the podium. They ascended the steps. Claude introduced the Patriarch to Prince Philip. I saw the Patriarch assuming Claude's place, the comfortable seat on the sofa next to Prince Philip. Prince Philip and he were now chatting – the situation had turned harmonious.

The next day, Claude explained his diplomatic feat.

'The solution was [to ask] one VIP Greek to [speak to and to host] another VIP Greek,' quipped Claude…

Fundraising

52

Let's Get Them

Rome, Italy

We had gathered in Rome, the Eternal City. The occasion? It was a WWF International Board of Trustees' annual meeting, with HRH Prince Philip acting as president and chair. Initially, the meeting was planned to be in Sardinia but an unexpected strike by Alitalia had meant a hasty change of venue. Rome was selected instead.

Twenty people attended the meeting and since Prince Philip was with us, we received special attention from the Roman authorities. For our sake, the members of the City Council of Rome had forsaken their customary meeting venue. Usually they would meet at a prestigious location – the museum that's behind the famous building the local Romans call "The Typewriter" (it earned this name because, viewed from afar, it looks exactly that – a gigantic typewriter).

As I entered the meeting room my first impression was that the room was immense- as large as two average detached houses in the United Kingdom. It would be equivalent to someone taking two such buildings, joining them together and hollowing the interior to create one vast space. There were splendid oil paintings by Italian masters adorning its walls and ornate antique furniture. As I passed through the tall double doors at one end of the room, I saw, at the far end, a wall consisting of transparent glass panes – through which a well-tended outdoor garden was clearly visible. It was early summer and the grounds outside were not only immaculately looked after but also lush and extremely green.

When the board meeting started, Prince Philip welcomed the participants. As the meeting progressed, different subjects were tabled and discussed. At one point the group turned to the subject of budgets – income plans and the spending targets to be set for the coming year. As discussions ensued, up came the topic of fundraising

'All sources of income are important,' said one board member.

The conversation then evolved to a discussion on the different types of income – especially bequests from legacies, these being an important revenue source. Many in the room voiced their views, confirming the importance of legacies – these being amounts of money or other assets bequeathed to someone or to some organisation in a will. Such income can indeed be an important source of income. Whilst I was working at WWF, many a time I witnessed substantial legacies arriving. Sometimes they can even amount to millions of US dollars. I have personally encountered at least two instances whereby the bequests even exceeded ten million. There was also a somewhat unusual legacy, whereby WWF was left real estate, with just one condition to be fulfilled. It was that the organisation would need to properly care for the deceased's cats. In this particular case, lawyers as well as an animal welfare organisation were consulted and a solution was arrived at.

Listening attentively to the discussions was Prince Philip, who sat at the far end of the room with his back to the gardens. Two seats to his left sat McLain Stewart, one of the trustees. "Mac", as we all address him, is an important senior partner at McKinseys. Mac is from the US. He lives in the US and has always been helpful to the conservation cause – participating in and advising on, fundraising, as well as providing pro bono consultation to WWF on management issues. Although advanced in age, Mac is in good health. Everyone likes Mac and whenever he spoke, we would pay close attention to his comments. As the subject of legacies was being further explored, Mac decided he would address the board too. Softly but with clear authority, he affirmed the conclusions.

'Legacies are indeed important,' he said.

Various heads around the table nodded up and down in agreement.

'A large amount of funds can be raised – if we all work closely together to address legacies,' added Mac.

Heads again bobbed up and down.

'That being the case, I suggest that we – we the Trustees – we, too, should *all* work on legacies. Let's talk to the people we know – many of whom are rich and influential – especially those well advanced in age.'

Mac paused. Then he decided to inject some humour to an otherwise serious topic.

'Let's get them before it's too late!' exclaimed Mac.

But, at the exact instant that Mac finished speaking, I heard a loud crash. Together with his chair, Mac had collapsed noisily onto the floor. I was shocked, as were the other meeting participants. Mac had disappeared from view. Where he sat, there was but an empty space – a void – all that was left were a few pieces of paper scattered on the surface of the table.

"Let's get them before it's too late!" His famous last words resonated in my ears. Stunned, I felt immense sympathy for Mac – as did everyone else. An uncomfortable hush pervaded the entire room. I felt very sorry about the whole incident. Then, whilst I was still in a state of shock, I perceived a head, appearing over the edge of the conference table.

'Still here,' said Mac…

St James's Palace Dinner

I was in Hampstead, London, spending a weekend with my sister, Lin Cook. Lin's one of my four sisters. I come from a family of six children, which means, inclusive of my parents, we were a total of eight. When we were kids growing up in Malaysia, merely to go to the movies we had to travel in two cars. Our mum had a Renault Dauphine whilst father had a large American car: an eye-catching red and white Ford Fairlane that had "fins" as well as huge red tail lights. Lin is the eldest and she has spent most of her life living in London. She first arrived in the UK to attend boarding school when she was just fourteen. Lin's husband was the late British writer, actor and satirist, Peter Cook.

'And where will it be held?' Lin asked me, referring to the WWF fundraising dinner I had mentioned.

'At St. James's Palace,' I said.

St. James's is a palace with much historical background. It has been the setting for some of the most important events in the history of the British monarchy. For more than three hundred years it was the residence of English kings and queens. Even today it remains the ceremonial residence of the Sovereign, although Buckingham Palace became the official royal residence when Queen Victoria ascended the throne.

It was to this St. James's Palace that my sister and I arrived one summer evening. After crossing a small external courtyard with the peculiar name of Friary Court, we entered the main building of the palace. I saw that all guests were smartly dressed for the occasion – the men wore dark suits whilst the majority of the women arrived in long dresses. The evening's event had two goals – raising awareness for conservation issues and fundraising.

Once inside the palace, after we had ascended a flight of steps, we approached a large door that led to one of the reception rooms. Standing by the side of the door was Prince Philip. Upon arrival, guests patiently formed a queue. When their turn came to be in front of HRH, Prince Philip welcomed each person, taking the time to say a few words to each guest.

The invitees streamed into the reception area. We sipped cocktails and mingled. At the appointed time, we were asked to move to an adjoining room for dinner. To locate our assigned table, Lin and I consulted a large board on which were pinned a listing of names and detailed table plans. Eventually, we and everyone else, found our seats.

Seated at my table, two chairs to my right, was a businessman from Bangladesh. He told me he was involved in publishing and that a fair amount of his time was spent in Western Europe, London in particular. There was also a gentleman who was linked to a well-known South American mining family but, in particular, I recall the Italian countess sitting to my left. She was an elegant Milanese woman, probably in her fifties and she had arrived that same day from Italy. She had come with two of her female friends who were also present at our table. They had all made the journey to London especially for the WWF fundraising dinner. There was lively dinner table conversation.

'My friends and I, we're all from Milan. Do you go there sometimes?' she asked. 'You *must* contact me if ever you do come. Do you like opera? If you need tickets for *La Scala*, just call me. They're hard to come by but I know how to get them. It's absolutely no problem for me…' she added.

After the first course had arrived and we had eaten it, our discussions turned to sports.

'Oh, so you play tennis and you started playing golf too,' she said. 'I think you should only play tennis – better tennis, not golf. It suits you better. Golf: that's for older people. Tennis is a younger type of sport – more virile.'

No sooner had she finished her sentence than the whole room started to quieten down. It was as though a magic wand had been waved. Conversation instantly slowed and became more hushed. Then the chatter volume further reduced, to finally cease altogether. Complete silence enveloped the entire room. Prince Philip had just walked to and ascended, the low podium that was set up against the wall in the middle of the room.

He first looked around the room. He took the microphone.

'Ladies and gentlemen, good evening. Thank you for attending our event this evening.' Then, pausing a second for effect, he continued.

'In case you do not already know, we are WWF. And what's our main activity? It's to invite and to offer you, the rich and famous, excellent dinners at inexpensive rates…'

Insider's View

London, England

During summer, once a week, huge crowds gather in front of Buckingham Palace. They are there to see the daily changing of the guards: a colourful ceremony. All the guards are impeccably dressed in their red tunics and wear bearskin hats. They stand to attention whilst the military band plays. Renderings by the band might vary from military marches to Abba's greatest hits – and, of course, "Happy Birthday" during royal birthdays. This is the Buckingham Palace picture-postcard London scene that attracts tourists by the masses.

It so happened that this ceremony also interested a member of one of WWF's more important donor families. This donor was from a wealthy family, as the late patriarch, who had strong Brazilian connections, had founded an important Swiss-based banking group. One day, a lady family member called the WWF fundraising office.

'I'm going to London,' she said. 'I'm going with my grandchildren. I'd like to take them to see the changing of the guards.'

'That's a good idea,' a WWF fundraising colleague replied. 'They'll enjoy it. You can get the timetable from the London tourist office [these were pre-internet days]. I think, during summer, it's daily – at 11.30 a.m. Try to go early – there'll be lots of people,' the fundraiser added.

'You don't understand.'

'You did say the changing of the guards?'

'Yes, I want to take my grandchildren to Buckingham Palace. To view the changing of the guards but [seeing it] from the inside [of the Palace]…'

Valuation Method

Montreux, Switzerland

I was in Montreux, attending a WWF annual conference. During the evening scheduled for the "family dinner" (meaning for WWF employees and related persons only, without any outside guests), I had consciously looked out for colleagues I had not yet met. Having selected a group, I walked over to them. I introduced myself and that was how I found myself amidst WWF Austria employees. WWF being a global network, participants had come from all over the world. This particular group were all from the Vienna office. We had been discussing financial matters when one of them nudged a colleague and said, 'Tell him about the bundle we received,' referring to me as the "him".

The WWF Austria colleague spoken to picked up the ball.

'Have you heard the story of the two kilos we received?' he said.

'You received two thousand dollars?' I said.

'No, I mean two kilos – we received two kilos.'

'I don't get it,' I said.

And the man explained.

'I'm usually the first one in the office. One morning, upon arrival, I found a pile of papers dumped on our doorstep. These papers were bunched together and tied tightly like a batch of old newspapers. Not knowing what they were, I took the whole stack into the office. I untied the bundle whereupon I realised they were documents. Each piece of paper looked official – and had "bearer" or "securities" or similar official wording written on it. Not knowing what to do with the pile, I put the bunch on a scale and I weighed it. The lot came to two kilos…'

His Big Toe

Geneva, Switzerland

For an organisation such as WWF to function, funds are needed. During the initial years of WWF, starting from 1961, the year when the organisation was founded, funding primarily came in the form of donations from individuals. I joined WWF International in 1991. At that time, "new" funding sources, such as income from corporations, was limited in amounts and somewhat frowned upon. There was, however, something illogical in the reasoning that funding from governments was deemed "OK", but not funding from corporations. Governments, after all, obtain a substantial amount of their funding via taxes levied on corporations or on individuals who are in turn employed by corporations.

The early 1990s was also the period during which WWF ventured to solicit more and therefore received greater funding amounts, from governments and aid agencies – these being termed internally as "GAA", meaning Governments and Aid Agencies' income sources. Some examples of GAA funding:

This could mean funding from the Swiss government via their development aid agency or from other aid agencies, be it from the US, the UK, Denmark, Sweden, France or the Netherlands, to name but a few.

Over the years, WWF became increasingly more comfortable with corporate funding and that is now an important income contributor too. However, income arising from individual donations remains a primary income source. Funding from corporations, although now considered acceptable, does generally involve certain restrictions and conditions before WWF is able to accept such funding. For example, donations from corporations involved in environmentally damaging industries are, in principle, ruled out. At times, heated debates arise as to whether a particular corporation passes, or does not fulfil, the stringent rules for accepting monies that have been set in place. In certain cases it's clear. For example, donations from a corporation involved in an extractive industry, such as mining, or a company engaged in the oil and gas sector, is generally considered not acceptable. Corporations involved in certain other industries, for example, airlines, automatically result in intensive discussions within WWF – some National Organisations, referred to within WWF as "NOs", find funding from such sources suitable, whilst other NOs are violently opposed. An example of airline funding is funding from Air France/KLM.

Another interesting example is funding from the Coca Cola Corporation. Some NOs find it acceptable as the funding from that company includes a programme to help improve the corporation's use of water. However, there are other NOs that do not agree to accept such funds. Their logic might be that the company uses too much water in the first place – not to mention the energy consumed for the distribution of the drinks. It can also sometimes happen that even if the funding is agreed upon, the detailed implementation might result in heated discussions. For example, one of the agreements made with Coca Cola was that they would be one of the sponsors for the WWF annual conference in Beijing. One of the events during that annual conference week was that guests and WWF colleagues were to meet (to listen to speeches by officials) at the Great Hall in Beijing, a prestigious location. That event started and finished without a hitch. However, unknown to most participants, there was much debating behind the scenes. Why was that? It was because Coca Cola wanted to have their red and white vending machines placed in the reception area so that arriving guests could clearly see and perhaps even use them if they so wished. The Coca Cola executives thought it was a good idea. However, WWF and the Chinese officials did not feel that such action would be appropriate – a clear case of cultural differences. In the end, the company gave in and the vending machines were not displayed.

Over the years, as WWF's assets have grown, another category of income has come into being. This is funding from WWF's "own income sources". This can mean income from financial assets or royalty income arising from licensing contracts (for example, use of the WWF logo on stamps or on coin collections).

In summary, as the organisation has grown, WWF's sources of income have evolved. From an initial narrow base of donations arising from individuals, it now has income from various other sources: from corporations, governments and aid agencies, from trusts and foundations, as well as "own income".

Revenue from individuals might mean a small amount collected by school kids. It could also mean funds from some of the many programmes that WWF runs, whereby supporters become "friends" or have some other descriptive titles given to them. Amounts can range from the small coins collected from travellers' loose change at airports to millions of dollars from wealthy individuals. All the different income sub-categories coming from individuals are important as they contribute to the total income and it is not uncommon to find individuals "progressing" from being one kind of contributor to then becoming another type, on a higher scale. For example, a schoolboy might be supporting a WWF programme using some of his pocket money. In later years, the same person might become a professional or a wealthy businessman who continues his support but at a different and more substantial level. Additionally, he is likely to introduce his children to the conservation cause.

In terms of my role to help support funding from individuals, I was not involved in those events that included a large number of people – a lot of people who contribute a small amount each so that the total does then become important. An example would be an organised charity run, whereby each runner has enlisted one or more sponsors. In those kinds of events I did not much participate. However, I was many a time involved in having contact with some of the wealthy individual donors, as they often had questions about the finances of the organisation. And since I was the Director of Finance and because I have been with WWF many years, I could answer most, if not all, of the questions raised.

Over the years, I had many encounters with individuals on fundraising matters. Some of the meetings I remember well.

An example follows:

'I'll arrange a meeting,' Eric Sarasin said to me. We had been discussing possible donations from a potential major donor. Eric was Treasurer of WWF International. A private banker, he fits perfectly the stereotype image of the Swiss private banker. Educated and well mannered, Eric's the elegant man-about-town. His many "hats" included his position as the CEO of private banking at Bank Sarasin (since taken over by Bank Safra), a reputable Swiss private bank based in Basel, founded by Eric's family many generations ago and which bears his family's name.

'He's one of the trustees. The foundation he manages is really sizeable,' Eric added.

Then, as I was leaving, Eric said, 'Let's meet at "le Cercle" – Editha (he was referring to Editha Rieder, his personal assistant) will e-mail you the date. It'll be a lunch.'

The Cercle de la Terrasse is a Swiss restaurant located in the old town of Geneva. In English, the restaurant's name translates as the "Terrace Circle". It's a private dining club, much frequented by bankers. It has, not surprisingly, given its name, a terrace adjacent to a garden. It's a pleasant lunch venue in summer and, given that restaurants with green space are not that plentiful in the old town of Geneva, the restaurant is appreciated by many. In addition to common areas for lounging, reading a newspaper or having a meal, the place also has private dining rooms. In terms of atmosphere it could best be described as a Swiss version of UK dining clubs. Located discreetly in a street with the almost impossible to remember name of Rue Jean-Gabriel Eynard, this luncheon club plays on understatement as a theme. There are no door name signs to indicate its existence. Only those in the know are aware that "No 4" is where it is. I have been there a few times. The food there is acceptable, although by no means exceptional – reasonably decent fare as one would find in many Geneva restaurants.

A few days after my conversation with Eric, whilst back at WWF International in Gland (Switzerland), I dropped into a colleague's office. It was the office of Chris Hails.

'Chris, I need you to join us,' I said.

'Join who?'

'Eric and me.'

I explained to Chris my conversation with Eric. Chris is British and he's someone with extensive experience in conservation matters. At one time, he was a lecturer at the University of Malaya. That was before the country became Malaysia. He had spent many years in Kuala Lumpur, prior to relocating to Switzerland as Director of Conservation at WWF International. Being knowledgeable and articulate, Chris can be very convincing. I therefore wanted him to be a key team member for the pending fundraising discussions. In terms of professional qualifications,

Chris is an ornithologist. 'I'm but a bird-man,' he would say.

The appointed day arrived and on to Geneva's old town we headed. I drove to Geneva and parked near the luncheon club. Leaving the vehicle, we walked the rest of the way. Upon arrival I rang the doorbell and a woman let us in. We ascended the stairs to reach the first floor of the restaurant-club. We entered one of the private dining rooms. Upon entering, I saw that Eric and the potential donor had arrived ahead of us. Eric stood up and introduced us to the guest, a British man, probably in his forties. Chris and I sat down. Eric retook his seat. He was seated next to the man, with Chris and myself facing them. Leaning slightly over the polished mahogany dinner table, Eric poured Chris and me some still water. Then he resumed conversing with the donor. Initially we talked about the weather and this was followed up by an exchange of views on current world affairs.

The meal was French. During lunch, Chris presented WWF's conservation goals and achievements. We engaged in discussions about environmental matters.

When we had finished the main course, Chris addressed the potential donor.

'If I may ask you – what donation amounts might your foundation be considering?' Chris said.

Chris had made the "ask", but he had recieved no response. The potential donor acted as though he had not heard the question. Clearly, he had no intention of replying. Instead, he skilfully sidestepped the query by asking even more questions about deforestation.

The man knew what he wanted and in this case also what he did not. Chris, wisely, did not persist. Fundraising is a fine art. Fundraisers are expected to ask. This is because most donors anticipate that they will be solicited. However, as to when the actual request is to be made, the precise timing is crucial. Not too early and yet not too late. By not insisting, Chris had made the right decision – to wait, until the donor was ready.

Shortly, we approached the end of our lunch. Dessert had been served and eaten. The waitress knocked on the closed door. She re-entered the room, arriving with coffee and biscuits. Chris and I glanced at each other. Has it now come? Was it now the opportune time to bring up again the subject of donations?

Just then, as we were pondering the matter, the guest answered our question.

'I like what WWF is doing. Our foundation will help,' he said.

We listened intently. We did not interrupt.

'In terms of funding – I suggest we start small. Over the years we can increase. As we gain confidence in WWF, our commitment can then grow.'

From experience, I know "starting small" is never a problem. Cultivating donors and establishing relationships requires patience and I have seen cases when initial small amounts have evolved over time to become substantial.

The potential donor continued, 'Yes, let's start slowly. You know, our foundation has vast financial resources but in terms of people working on it, there are not many staff. In fact there's only my wife and me and we review project proposals over the kitchen table. We like to take the time to get to know the organisations we support. And then, over the years, gradually grow our commitment.'

Eric, Chris and I continued to listen politely.

The potential donor continued, 'Let's commence the process by dipping one toe in the water.'

I held my breath as I waited for him to articulate the amount.

'Yes, a toe to start with will be fine, say, a quarter of a million pounds…'

57

Panda Gown

Singapore

They stood next to each other, Princess Laurentien, wife of Prince Constantjin, third son of Queen Beatrix of the Netherlands and Charlene of Monaco. Both smiled gracefully whilst multiple flashbulbs popped. Various photographs were taken, of which some were with a giant panda posing next to them – the giant panda being one of the WWF Singapore colleagues dressed in a Panda outfit.

This occurred during an afternoon, in one of the reception rooms of the St Regis Singapore hotel. Charlene (at that time without the title of "Princess" as she hadn't yet married Prince Albert) had travelled to Singapore, to attend the evening's function – WWF's Asian Panda Ball.

What's the WWF Asian Panda Ball?

Following the success of Panda Balls in Europe, WWF decided to clone the event in Asia. The logic for doing so is that Asia as a region is developing rapidly. With its high economic growth rate and a fast increasing population, Asia will surely be playing an increasingly important role on conservation matters. That being the case, it made sense to build up conservation awareness in Asia, and thus WWF would be establishing the platform for future conservation efforts, including fundraising activities. To achieve these goals, one of the tools would be the holding of annual Panda Balls, this time an Asian equivalent.

Choosing between Shanghai and Singapore as possible venues, the final choice came down to Singapore, where WWF had opened offices some three years back. HRH Prince Philip had performed the opening ceremony. This he did whilst on his return trip from a state visit when he accompanied the Queen to Australia.

For the ball, Prince Albert of Monaco had been solicited to be the guest of honour. Aware of his sympathy to the conservation cause and knowing of his nautical interests (Singapore is much involved with shipping matters), WWF concluded he would be the ideal guest of honour. The prince, however, had declined. This was because the dates we had proposed clashed with one of his other commitments, Monaco's National Day. As an alternative, palace officials had replied that Charlene would represent the prince. And that was how it came about on that afternoon that there was Charlene and Princess Laurentien of the Netherlands, both posing for the press. Also attending that evening's events were two other princesses, from Bali and from Cambodia – although they were not present during that afternoon's photographic session.

When the session was over, I left the room to explore the hotel. Arriving at the lobby area I came across some fundraising colleagues.

One of them, Alexandra Dauphin, waved to me, 'Come join us. We've a problem – maybe you'll know what to do,' she said.

Alexandra was at that time events manager at WWF International. As part of her responsibilities, she would organise functions such as the Panda Ball. She's Swiss, someone with a positive outlook in life and a captivating quick smile.

'If I can help – what's the problem?' I said.

'You recall the evening gown Charlene wore in Monaco?' she said

'Yes, the one with the panda,' I said.

'There's a problem,' she said

'Come again?' I said

'The palace donated it for auction.'

'So?'

'We're not sure what to do with it. We can't say no thanks, we don't want it.'

'So, you keep the dress.'

'Yes, but when we auction it – will we find any takers?'

'And why not?' I asked.

A male colleague replied to me via mime. He placed both his hands in front of his chest and made a curving gesture, miming breasts.

'People here have small sizes,' he said

'I see,' I said.

A female colleague added, 'And even if we have bids – they must be substantial. Otherwise it would be an embarrassment. Not only for the palace but also vis-à-vis Charlene – since she'll be attending the dinner.'

After some discussions, I proposed a solution that was immediately seized upon. I volunteered my sister's help, knowing that she would agree. Lin had flown in from London and had sponsored a table. I was to arrange with her and with Bee Yeow, one of her female friends, that they get involved with the bidding that evening. The goal was to ensure that bids reach a decent minimum. This way, whatever happened, bids or no bids from the public, "face" would be saved.

The evening soon arrived and the Asian Panda Ball commenced. Speeches were delivered and dinner was served. Towards the latter part of the evening, the auction started. As the sale progressed, lot after lot was systematically sold off but still no sight of the gown.

'When will that be?' my sister asked.

'Be patient,' I said.

Finally, as we were being served dessert, the turn of the gown arrived.

'And now, ladies and gentlemen, we have a fabulous evening gown to offer you,' the auctioneer said.

He pointed to the evening gown that someone had just brought onto the stage.

He then directed our attention to the big screen that projected various photographs of an elegant Charlene wearing the gown.

'Ready for the bid?' Bee Yeow whispered to Lin.

'Yes.'

And the auction commenced.

Lin made a bid.

One of Lin's other friends at the table was much surprised to see her bid.

'What do you want the dress for?' she said.

That friend was then even more surprised to next see Bee Yeow upping Lin's bid.

However, her surprise was nothing compared to the disbelief expressed on the face of Tuck Onn, Bee Yeow's husband.

But Lin and Bee Yeow did not have to bid alone. Other bids came pouring in – thick and fast. There was no let-up. It was like the first day of sales at Harrods. Quickly, the final bid reached an important the amount and it was sold off for around ten thousand US dollars. At the precise instant when the auctioneer's hammer came crashing down with a loud bang, I could not help myself. Instantly, I glanced at the winning bidder's bosom. To this day, I'm not sure she bought the correct dress size…

152

PART SEVEN

153

Business Unusual

58

Monsieur, She's French

Paris, France

I was having lunch in a French restaurant with Raj Nair, an Indian friend, in Geneva.

'I don't think I'll take it up,' I said. We had been discussing Swiss citizenship. 'It's too expensive.'

It was during the early 1980s when I made those comments. In those days, any foreign male married to a Swiss woman was required to pay a fee if he wanted to acquire Swiss nationality. The amount payable included not only a percentage of income but also a percentage of wealth. The foreign man had to first make the necessary application, then go through a series of processes and, if successful, the final step would be the payment. However, in the case of any foreign woman married to a Swiss man, none of the complicated rules were applicable and there was no payment due. This was unfair in terms of equal treatment of the sexes but then it is to be remembered that Swiss women were only given the right to vote in 1971. That was when 600,000 of the all-male electorate voted "yes" – however, some 300,000 still voted "no".

I did not then apply for a Swiss passport, nor did Raj. Payment aside, I was discouraged by the fact that there were all those hurdles to pass. Obstacles included knowing the national anthem and having sufficient knowledge of Swiss history. It was further rumoured that the Swiss police were performing checks on applicants. These stories were further fed when a satirical movie, *The Swiss Makers,* was released. The movie portrayed over-zealous Swiss immigration officers pursuing rigorous checks on applicants, including making surprise visits to applicants' homes. Due to these reasons, neither Raj nor I applied for Swiss citizenship.

Years later, the rules substantially changed.

'You know, I only had to fill in a form, attend a short interview and that was it,' Raj said.

'That simple?' I said.

'My citizenship papers arrived in the post. It's that easy now. And no fee was asked for.'

'How interesting.'

The following week, I completed and sent off the application forms for Swiss citizenship.

I had no news from the authorities for a few months. Then, one winter's day, I received a letter. I was asked to attend an interview at the police station in Nyon, a small town near Geneva. The date was given and the time specified as "at 0800 hours".

When the appointed morning arrived, I looked out the window. It was white everywhere as it had been snowing all night and it was still snowing. My Jaguar was not even visible as it was entirely covered with snow. That particular day, although it was winter, my car still had summer tyres on. I should have already equipped the car with snow ones but had not yet done so.

Driving at a snail's pace as the roads were snow-covered and after what seemed an eternity, I finally arrived at the police station. I drove my car into the designated parking area and entered the building. The constable in charge of my citizenship application file greeted me. He was a jovial man. He led me to a small meeting room. He told me that the interview was part of the process and no, I need not worry. There would neither be tough drilling nor trick questions. He assured me everything would be straightforward. And the interview started.

'How long have you lived in Switzerland?' he asked.

This was followed by various other "tough" questions such as:

'What are your hobbies?'

'Where do you work?'

'Do you like living here?'

In fact the entire interview was a friendly chat.

After half an hour the interview terminated and I left.

Back to the car park I went. I found more snow had fallen. I entered my car. I tried to reverse the Jaguar but could make no headway. The wheels kept spinning in a void. After a few futile attempts, I gave up. I left the car and re-entered the police station. I asked to speak with my interviewer. The man was most sympathetic. Within minutes, he had enlisted two other policemen and they accompanied me to my car. They aligned themselves behind my car and they pushed my Jaguar, together with its inappropriate summer tyres, back onto the main road. And that was the morning I applied to be Swiss, on my way to work.

Years later, a proud Swiss citizen by then, who also received his papers through the post, I attended a conference on responsible investments, held in Paris. This particular conference occurred in a convent. This was because the organisers had close links with a charity that had ties with a church. A peculiarity of this convent is that it also houses a nursing home for the elderly.

During the mid-morning coffee break, I left the meeting room and walked along a corridor adjacent to a garden. Whilst I was there I saw an elderly French lady approaching. She was small and looked frail but had an alert look in her eyes. For support, she held on to the arm of a black nurse. Step by slow limping step, the old lady and the nurse walked along the corridor towards where I stood. I could see they were both chatting. They obviously got on well with each other.

Then they were right next to me.

'Bonjour, monsieur,' said the old lady.

'Bonjour, madame,' I replied.

'Do you know… monsieur. Do you know, she's French?' she said, haltingly in French, referring to the nurse standing beside her.

The black nurse must have been telling her about her French nationality. She, being of an older generation, was probably not used to the concept – and apparently bemused she had made that comment to me.

'Yes, madame, I know. And do you know, I'm Swiss?' I said…

59

Pecking Order

Vienna, Austria

When it comes to food, perhaps we humans can be compared to chickens – we have a pecking order. This too was the case at WWF. Whenever we had events with food being served, there was a sequence in terms of who ate first. This is of course a consequence of cultural backgrounds, generally accepted norms of politeness and the relative importance of the attendees.

On several occasions and especially if it was a buffet meal with HRH Prince Philip present, we would all wait for him to start. The food would be laid out on long tables and would look sumptuous. The waiters and waitresses would be there, impeccable in their uniforms and ready to serve guests, but no one would ever make a beeline for the food. Everyone would wait until HRH commenced. Then and only then, did others follow suit. Similarly, at the end of a dinner, when HRH stood up and left, we all knew the evening had come to a close.

Always waiting for HRH to start made me wonder about the ranking order of European royalty. It so happened that a couple of months later I was at a fundraising dinner in Vienna, sitting next to a person who was able to explain it to me.

As we were having dinner, one of my neighbours told me she was a viscountess.

'I've never met a viscountess – does that mean your husband's a viscount?' I said.

'Yes, that's correct.'

'But what's a viscount? Is there an official ranking for the different titles?'

'Would you like me to explain?'

'Yes, that would be interesting.'

She then explained to me the different titles, in ascending order, as follows:

    Baron   Baroness
    Viscount   Viscountess
    Count   Countess
    (A count is also referred to as an earl)
    Marquis   Marchioness
    Prince   Princess
    Duke   Duchess
    King   Queen

And that summer evening, sitting on the terrace of a restaurant in Vienna, was when I had a quick lesson concerning the "pecking order" of European aristocracy.

60

City Bankers

London, England

Certain WWF country offices, particularly those in developed countries, hold reserve funds. Such funds would typically be invested by an investment manager or, if the amounts held were substantial, by investment managers. At the same time, an investment committee would be established to set investment policy, as well as to steer and monitor the managers.

This too was the case for WWF UK. Asset managers had been hired and an investment committee had been set up. Heading the committee at one time was Jeremy Edwards, a retired corporate executive. Jeremy had previously been the Chief Executive Officer of Hendersons, investment managers based in the UK.

One morning, I was on the telephone, discussing investments with Les Jones, Finance Director of WWF UK.

'You know, it'll be good if you attend one of our Investment Committee meetings. Why not come join us for the next one? This way you'll see for yourself, first-hand, how we work,' he said.

The meeting was scheduled to be in London. We were to meet with investment managers of X-Corporation (not its real name), one of WWF UK's two asset managers. We were to convene at their posh offices in the City.

On the appointed day, although I arrived early, I found that my WWF colleagues were already there in full force, sitting at the reception area. I joined them and we waited. Shortly, a secretary arrived. She led us to the boardroom. I noticed, at one end of the room, a large mirror on the mantelpiece. Bordered by an elaborate gold frame, it was sparkling clean. Next to it was a table where silver trays filled with tasty-looking sandwiches had been laid out. There was a stack of expensive looking small porcelain plates, crystal glasses, silverware and bottles of water, both still and sparkling. Everything was elegantly displayed.

When the three executives of X-Corporation arrived, Jeremy introduced them to me. Greetings and niceties were exchanged.

'Please help yourselves to the sandwiches so that we may start,' one of the bankers said.

I took a plate and helped myself to two shrimp sandwiches. I opted for still water. The bankers did not take any food.

We sat around the long and gleaming mahogany conference table. The three bankers took their seats, facing us. They started their presentation. I began to eat my sandwiches. I tried to do it quietly.

Taking turns to speak, the bankers commented upon factors that would contribute to the strength and to the weakness of the British pound. They did the same for the US dollar. They commented upon George Bush Senior's foreign policies. Following that, they commented upon the state of political affairs in the Middle East. After a seemingly long half hour, they were still making general comments about world affairs. Then they started to give their views concerning future expectations for the stock market. Those views, however, were mostly what I would describe as comments of no practical use. Their remarks were what I would call "two-way" bets. It was tantamount to saying that it will be a dry day tomorrow, *if* it does not rain. We were treated to phrases such as: 'We think the US dollar could (note, "could", not that it necessarily "will") weaken in the long term, but in the short term, it may (note, "may" not "will") remain strong.'

I found the presentations thoroughly uninteresting. Often, investment managers do present the macro economic picture, as part of their meeting with clients. A portion of time spent on such issues can sometimes be interesting. However, that day, their presentation on world politics and general economic matters was getting a bit long-winded and tedious.

I became impatient.

'I know you are still making the macro presentation. But I have a question – what do the [investment results] numbers look like?' I said.

'Actually, we didn't bring any numbers,' said one of the bankers.

I almost fell off my chair.

Jeremy, being the polite gentleman that he is, expressed his disappointment. He did it in a respectful and civil way. The bankers, in turn, apologised. They blamed the situation on software problems. As there was then nothing more to say at that stage, they bade us goodbye and left the room.

We remained in the boardroom.

'I had beforehand agreed with them that we can continue to use their boardroom for our committee meeting,' Jeremy explained to me.

'This is supposed to be a reputable City firm of investment managers. How can they do that – arrive with no numbers?' I said.

'Not only that, this was not the first time,' Jeremy said…

61

Blow It All Out

Paris, France.

'That'll be interesting. I'll come,' I said to Marion de Marcillac. Marion used to work for WWF France. She had been telling me about after-work meditation sessions. I of course know about after-work drinks but after-work meditation; that was something new. I decided to give it a try.

'Here's the address. If you go, you'll likely find me there too. The nearest metro is Chateau Landon. It starts at half-past seven. Or we can go together. Why don't you meet me at La Ruche,' she said, referring to the offices where she worked, called La Ruche, meaning "The Hive", in Quai de Jemmapes.

'I'll come too,' said Carole Mihilewicz, my assistant.

The next day, Carole and I set off to meet Marion. Having met up, the three of us walked alongside the Canal Saint Martin. It was seven in the evening. There was still light as it was early summer. After fifteen minutes, we found ourselves on Passage Delessert, a small street where the meditation session was to be held.

'Do I have to pay?' I asked Marion.

'No, there's no fee payable. But on your way out you might want to leave five euros in the cardboard box.'

Entering the building, we removed shoes and headed to the room where attendees were to meditate. There were already about twenty people in the small room. They were mostly French. I noticed a low podium at the end of the room. Behind it were small, tacky-looking multi-coloured light bulbs. On the platform was a small gold-coloured sitting-Buddha statue and hanging on the walls were Buddhist scrolls as well as Tibetan symbols. The burning joss sticks emitted a smell I did not like, although joss sticks burning on the family altar had been an everyday event in my parents' home. I never got accustomed to them, always having felt that it could not be healthy to inhale all that smoke.

At twenty past seven the monk arrived. He was French, of medium height and was neither fat nor thin. Bespectacled, he was dressed in crumpled saffron-coloured robes. He was probably in his forties but it was hard to tell. He did not have much hair. He seemed a nice chap. He walked to the front of the room and took his place on the podium, sitting cross-legged, facing all of us.

We assumed our places on the floor mats, crossing our legs like him and facing him. Even I somehow managed that pose, although not without some discomfort.

I listened attentively and silently when the monk started. He spoke softly, in French. It was ironic. There I was, a Chinese man, taking meditation lessons from a French monk but I had to admit that he was good. In fact, he was very good. He was serene and was most clear with his instructions.

Looking calmly at us he said, 'Attachments are the cause of suffering. Attachments, be it to things or to people – in fact, all kinds of attachments. To be rid of suffering, you need to free yourself of attachments. We shall now practise the movements that remove attachments. I'll show you how. Take the second finger of your right hand. Place it on top of your nose and press down so that you block your right nostril. Slowly, breathe in through your left nostril. Take your time.'

I did that and air went in through my left nostril.

'Hold your breath. Now using the same finger, press down to block your left nostril instead. Next, as you breathe out, imagine you are blowing out all attachments. Attachments cause suffering. So blow them *all* out.'

As he said that, I considered his comments. Life has its ups and downs but on the whole, I have a reasonably pleasant life. And yes, I'm attached to some things and to some people. Yet I know what he had said made sense. Now I was told to blow it all out, all my attachments. Do I really want to do that?

Pondering over what the monk had said, I decided to heed his advice. Through my right nostril I slowly blew out the air, but not all of it…

Foreign Languages

Zeist, Netherlands

I was in a car with Henner Ehringhaus. He and I were both sitting in a taxi in Zeist, in the Netherlands, on the way to the WWF offices, when it started to drizzle. Then the rain started to really pour down. I was gazing at the rainwater streaming along the taxi windows, when Henner asked me a question.

'Do you speak Dutch?'

'No,' I said.

'It's useful to know foreign languages.'

'Of course, but why are you telling me this?'

'There was a mouse family. There was Daddy Mouse, Mummy Mouse and their two kids – a boy and a girl. Hiding behind a small hole in the wall, Mummy Mouse and the kids were shivering with fear. Just on the other side was a large, menacing tomcat. It kept peering into the hole and with one paw it was clawing at it.

They called for Daddy Mouse. He rushed to the scene. The kids trembled, fearful of what might shortly be their fate – unsure if their dad could handle the situation. But Daddy Mouse was cool and confident.

"Don't worry, all of you. I'll sort him out. All I ask is that you keep quiet," he said. He then went next to the hole. He unbuttoned his shirt. He loosened his tie. He cleared his throat. Then, in as deep a voice as he could muster, he went, "Woof! Woof!"

The startled cat recoiled and ran off. Daddy Mouse turned to face his family.

"Kids, don't ever forget: foreign languages are useful," he said.'

His Ego Trip

Stockholm, Sweden

At the request of the Chief Executive Officer of WWF Sweden, I flew to Stockholm to discuss financial matters. The meetings went well. It would normally have been another routine business trip but no, that was not the case, as I found out later, when I boarded my plane to return to Geneva.

'Welcome on board,' the air hostess had greeted me. Although there were many of us boarding the aircraft, the process did not take long. The plane quickly filled up. I seated myself on my allotted aisle seat and started to read the newspaper I had brought with me. Ten minutes elapsed but the plane had not moved. By the time I finished reading my newspaper, a further ten minutes had passed by and our plane still had not budged. By now we had much overrun our scheduled departure time – and yet strangely enough, there was no explanatory announcement on the intercom.

I saw the pilot talk to one of the seated passengers. Prior to that, I had also witnessed two of the hostesses, as well as the chief steward, having discussions with the same man. Surely something was amiss. Why would so many airline staff approach this particular person?

I endured a further tedious quarter of an hour's wait. Some of my fellow passengers became agitated. It being a Friday evening, they were in a hurry to return home to commence their weekend.

As one of the stewardesses walked by, a passenger asked her what was going on.

'Yes, there's a problem, sir. But don't worry, sir. We're working on it,' she said.

So I heard it confirmed that indeed there was a problem. An issue probably linked to the aforementioned passenger, although I have to admit that he looked quite normal. Dressed in a dark business suit, he did not seem much different from the rest of us.

Two burly uniformed men arrived. They went directly to the man.

'They've come to arrest him or to throw him out,' I said to my neighbour.

The security officers conversed with the passenger. They did not produce any handcuffs. There was not the slightest sign of any violence. After a few minutes, they left the plane.

The clock ticked. A half hour went by. Another of the by now extremely unhappy passengers asked a stewardess for news.

'The captain – he's sorting things out, sir. He'll shortly make an announcement,' she said.

Incredibly, only after a further two long hours, finally, one of the airline crew closed the plane's door.

'Ouf,' sighed my neighbour.

'You can say that again. Finally we are leaving but what on earth was the delay all about?' I said.

Our plane slowly taxied away from the parking area.

Suddenly, the previously very silent public announcement system rumbled as it broke into life.

'Ladies and gentlemen, this is your captain. Please accept my apologies for the long wait. It's most unusual. But this lateness was beyond our control. I had to delay our flight. We had an unfortunate incident linked to one of our passengers.'

'Must be that chap,' my neighbour said.

The captain continued.

'Per aviation rules, all dogs exceeding a certain size must travel in the hold, the cargo area. This is per safety regulations. This evening, one of our passengers boarded our plane, together with his dog. Although still small, but exceeding the maximum allowed size, his dog should travel in the hold – but the passenger refused.'

My neighbour shook his head in disbelief.

'This gentleman turned down our suggestion to have his dog moved to the hold. He also flatly refused to vacate the plane. So I was left with only one choice: to delay the flight until his dog left the cabin area. We tried repeatedly to convince this passenger. Finally, as a last resort, I contacted senior management and asked for guidance. At first they were unsure as to what to advise. But just a few minutes ago, I received an unwelcome telephone call. My bosses instructed me, in fact, to be more precise, ordered me, to fly this plane. To take-off, even though the passenger refused to have his dog leave the cabin.'

Our captain sounded really unhappy. He paused for a fraction of a second. Then he continued.

'Against all rules I am therefore doing as told. Ladies and gentlemen, you might wonder – why did my management give in? Well, it's because the passenger in question is someone important in the travel business. He owns many travel agencies and is considered to be a VVIP – a Very Very Important Person. Ladies and gentlemen, if I may ask you – to please never bring a dog into the cabin. But should you absolutely need to do so, please, please [he repeated himself on purpose] do make sure you are a VVIP.'

Swiss Watches

In the skies

In Geneva, I boarded my plane and headed for seat 20C. From experience, I knew it would be an aisle seat and to my right as I walked in. I arrived at the row of three seats. Already seated there, on seat 20A, was a young woman. I slung my travel bag inside the overhead storage compartment and took my seat.

'*Bonjour*,' I greeted the female occupant of 20A.

She seemed rather young.

'Are you a student?' I asked.

'Oh no, I'm not that young but thanks for the compliment. I'm a journalist.'

'Journalist for?'

'I specialise in two topics: finance and Swiss watches.'

'That's an unusual combination. Are you now on a financial or a Swiss watch business mission? Or is this a personal trip?'

'My magazine's been invited by Hublot [Swiss watch manufacturers] for a product launch.'

'For such an invite, do they pay for everything? Excuse me for asking, I'm just curious.'

'No problem – yes, they pay for everything.'

She looked at my left wrist.

'What watch are you wearing?' she said.

'An Omega – interesting you ask. No one has ever noticed this watch. It has low-key looks but in fact it's my favourite.'

'I know about watches. That's why I'm asking you,' she said.

'When I was fifteen, I passed a glitzy shop window where I saw this watch displayed. Impressed with the chronograph and the dials, I felt I had to have it. I was then living in Asia. When I returned home, I told my mother about it. Being the doting mum she was, she promptly bought it for me. She's no longer alive now, my mother, but this watch from her remains. And you know, it still keeps perfect time.'

'That makes it even more special. May I have a look?'

I handed her my watch. She took it and inspected it. She turned it from side-to-side.

'Is Hublot sending someone to meet you at the airport?' I asked.

'Yes they are – they are thorough. It's all part of their sophisticated marketing machine.'

'Can you give me a lift to town? That would save my office the taxi fare.'

'And what do I tell the driver?'

'Just say I'm your bodyguard.'

'OK, bodyguard, it's a deal.'

Our plane landed and we left the aircraft together.

Exiting the customs area, I saw a man holding a large cardboard sign. The board had one single word, "Hublot", written on it. We greeted him. He told us we would need to wait, as there was one other person expected, also invited by Hublot.

Minutes later, another watch journalist, a man this time, joined us. We made our way to the car. Being the self-invited passenger, I volunteered to sit in front with the chauffeur.

As our car headed towards town, I turned to face the backseat passengers in order to converse with them. We engaged in small talk. After a few minutes of discussions, the newly arrived male watch journalist asked me a question.

'What's that watch you have?'

I laughed.

'I've been wearing this watch for years. Nobody ever notices it. It's anything but "bling-bling". But today, within two hours, I meet two people showing an interest in it.'

'May I see it?' he said.

'Sure,' I said.

I handed him my watch.

'Nice,' he said.

I told him about the shop window and my indulgent mum.

'Where are you from?' he asked.

'Malaysia. But I now live in Switzerland. I like it there, although on some cold winter days I wouldn't mind a few days in the sun. But I do travel frequently to Asia. Are you both Swiss?'

'Yes,' the two journalists replied simultaneously.

I decided to tell them about a Swiss watchmaker I met in Asia.

'Some years ago, during one of my trips to Malaysia, I accompanied my brother. He was going for an afternoon of jet skiing with a Swiss man, Rolf, who used to live there. Rolf told me he lived in Malaysia and that I got it all wrong by living in his native Switzerland. He said he swapped living in his cold country for a place in the sun – and asked how come I did the opposite. That was the late Rolf Schneider. The chap from Zurich who bought Ulysees Nardin and who then developed the brand.'

The male journalist grinned.

'My name's Louis Nardin. I'm from the family that sold Rolf the company,' he said.

As the car drove on, the three of us continued chatting and we had many a laugh, all the way during the drive to town. Shortly, we reached town. They dropped me off and I bade them goodbye.

The next day, my planned meetings progressed without a single hitch. At day's end, I boarded my plane for the return journey to Geneva.

I sat down on seat 22C, another aisle seat. Minutes later, a young man arrived. His was seat 22A. He was dressed in a dark business suit – obviously someone who worked in a corporation or a bank. I stood up to let him through. The man thanked me and he sat down. He was holding a huge coffee table type book that he laid upon his lap. With curiosity I looked at his book. It had a glossy cover. Splashed in large font on the cover was one single word –"Watches". It was an impressive-looking book.

We exchanged greetings. We chatted a bit and then, after a few minutes of polite conversation, he asked me a question.

'May I have a look at your watch?' he said…

Napoleonic Connections

In a Swiss train

We were both sitting in a Swiss train, travelling from Basel to Geneva. As expected, our train was running precisely on time. I was sitting with my back to the direction of travel, facing Jean-Paul Jeanrenaud. Jean-Paul's in his forties and he often sports a beard. He was, for almost twenty years, a colleague. Once in a while it could happen that we would be travelling together. This does not occur often, perhaps once every few years. Jean-Paul is someone intelligent, articulate and funny, with a wry sense of humour. He's British, has a very English accent, but also speaks perfect French.

'Where are you from?' I asked Jean-Paul. 'Your accent's English but Jean-Paul's not a British name,' I said.

'I'll explain,' he said. 'I was brought up in the UK. I had an English education, hence the accent. But through my French grandmother, we have a French connection.'

'I see.'

'Grandma now lives in France near the Swiss border. She once explained our family background. Our roots can be traced all the way back to Napoleonic days. In fact our lineage is directly linked to the Emperor himself.'

'Wow, that's something,' I said.

I continued to listen attentively. It's not often I hear about someone's Napoleonic connections. As the Swiss train continued moving and sceneries of the rolling hills and the lush Swiss countryside kept whizzing past our train's windows, Jean-Paul explained to me his Napoleonic link.

'Yes, grandma told me – we are descended from the bastard line of Napoleon,' he said...

Are Swiss Politicians Dull?

Geneva, Switzerland

Near Geneva railway station, less than five minutes' walk away, are some Credit Suisse offices. It was there I went for investment presentations organised by the bank. When I arrived reception staff welcomed me warmly and one of them led me to a medium-sized conference room. I surveyed the place and decided to occupy a vacant front row seat.

I said hello to my neighbour.

'I forget, who's the keynote speaker?' I asked.

'Pascal Couchepin, if I recall right,' my neighbour said, as he checked his papers.

'Let's see what he'll be telling us,' I said.

Pascal Couchepin is a successful Swiss politician. He was at one time even the President of Switzerland.

Right on time, the conference commenced.

Our banking hosts welcomed us. We were given an outline of the morning's programme. The keynote speaker was introduced.

Mr Couchepin ascended the podium. I had never met him before. He did not have much hair but had a sincere smile.

'My country, Switzerland, is a small country,' he said. 'We like to be left alone. Left alone so that we can get on with our business. That being the case, the more we are confused with other countries the better. As far as the rest of the world is concerned, please continue. Do mix us up with others as much as you like. Carry on being mistaken, confusing us with Sweden, with Senegal, with Swaziland…'

'He's funny,' said my neighbour.

'I agree,' I said.

Couchepin continued.

'This morning I came here to this meeting by train. I enjoyed the journey. There are benefits to no longer being in power. One big advantage is that I'm not anymore obliged to be chauffeured around in sedan cars. Previously, it was a case of black cars here and black cars there. I had no choice, not even for short trips. The irony is that on a nice sunny day, if I wanted to walk, I had to first ask the chauffeur for permission.'

'I like him,' said my neighbour.

After those jokes, Couchepin delved into the serious part of his presentation. He finished and he was followed by other speakers, as was planned, for the first part of the morning. Then came an intermission, the coffee break. I decided to go say hello to him.

I went up to him but he was already talking with someone else. When he had finished that conversation, I introduced myself.

'I found your "do carry on confusing us with other small countries" comments funny,' I said.

'Thank you and, if I may ask, where are you from?'

'I'm Chinese. My grandparents originate from China.'

'Ah, I see, China. As you know, we're a small country with a tiny population. Once, when I was on a state visit to China, the Chinese President asked me about the size of the Swiss population. You know what he said to me when I replied seven million?'

'No,' I said.

'Next time, please bring the whole family…'

67

Elephant God

Bombay, India

Meeta Yvas was at one time WWF India's general manager. Of Indian origin, she had spent some years in the United States after graduating from Columbia Business School. Following that, when she returned to her home country and started her new job with WWF India, she had contacted me. She had requested I visit India, to help her in her management review of some of the larger WWF India offices. These were offices located in towns such as Delhi or Bombay. That was how I found myself in Bombay, travelling in a taxi with Meeta, on our way to the local WWF office. It was a hot and humid morning.

We had hardly gone a hundred metres when our taxi driver slammed his right hand onto the middle of the car's steering wheel. Immediately, the horn hooted. He repeated the gesture. Like a maniac, he kept banging the palm of his hand on the steering wheel. In response and with no let-up, the drivers of the other cars all honked back. The commotion seemed perfectly normal to the different players although I found all that noise nerve-racking. In spite of the cacophony, the traffic somehow managed to inch along.

'I hope you like it, your first trip to India, although I know it's really hot,' Meeta said.

'I agree it's hot,' I said.

'It's the wrong season to be here. July's a bad month to be visiting us, so thanks again for agreeing to come,' she said.

'Glad if I can be of some help,' I said

'By the way, you must have seen some statues of our Indian gods?

'Yes, I have.'

'In India, we have many gods.'

'I know.'

'Did you notice Ganesh, the one with an elephant head?'

'I did – most unusual.'

'You know his story?'

'No.'

As she spoke, our taxi encountered more traffic. Our car, a model named "Ambassador", slowed. Meantime, the hooting continued relentlessly.

'Shiva – that's one of our male gods. One day, he met Parvati, a goddess. From their union, Parvati gave birth to a son, Ganesh,' she said.

'Ah, the elephant-headed god,' I said.

'That's correct. But although they were a couple, Shiva and Parvati lived apart. Shiva lived by himself, whilst Parvati lived with Ganesh in a cave. One day, an unexpected visitor arrived there – it was Shiva himself. Ganesh was guarding the cave's entrance when he arrived. Not knowing the caller was Shiva, he refused to let him in. Being a short-tempered god, Shiva raised his trident and beheaded Ganesh.'

'Wow, what a story,' I said.

'When Parvati arrived and saw the headless body, she wept. To make amends Shiva promised to restore Ganesh's head. He would use the head of the first living creature he came across. Shiva scrambled out of the cave and as he rushed out, Shiva came across his involuntary donor – an elephant. That's why our god Ganesh has an elephant's head.'

Thanks to Meeta, my noisy and confusing Bombay taxi ride was turned into an interesting education. I had learnt the story of Ganesh – the Indian god with the elephant head…

68

Samurai Warriors' Lot

Beijing, China

Years ago, whilst living in Malaysia, I had read and enjoyed James Clavell's Asian saga book, *Shogun*. With this book, I had travelled to ancient Japan. Therein were tales of samurai warriors, of the shogunate and, of course, of the shogun himself. Reading that book and thanks to latter-day Hollywood movies, I can easily conjure up images of imposing samurai fighters. They would be dressed in full battle gear, complete with elaborate headwear. When they attacked and especially if doing so on horseback, which was the case in one movie, they must have been an awe-inspiring sight.

When I boarded the bus, on the way to an official WWF function in Beijing and took a seat by the window, I was not to suspect who would soon be sitting next to me. Seconds after I sat down, a person took the seat next to me. We said hello to each other.

'My name's Tsunenari Tokugawa,' he said

He explained he was the board chairman of WWF Japan.

I made small talk with him.

After a few minutes of conversation, he brought up the subject of ancient Japan. 'Have you read the book, *Shogun*?' he said.

'Yes, I have. Why do you ask?'

'You know, I'm the eldest male descendant and therefore the [eighteenth] head of the Tokugawa shongunai household.'

The man wore no kimono that day. He had no menacing long samurai sword hanging from his waist. He had a stately bearing and did not look like a samurai – although I could well imagine him or his ancestors as shoguns. We did not have a long conversation. This was because our bus soon arrived at its destination and we left each other.

A few years later, I bumped into Tsunenari again. This time it was in Zurich.

'We didn't have time to finish our conversation when we last chatted,' I said. 'About shoguns and samurais – did your family ever write a book?' I asked.

'Actually, yes – I did write one,' he said.

'What's the book's title?'

'*The Edo Inheritance*,' he said.

Edo's the ancient name of Tokyo.

'Interesting. Is it in English? Can I buy it on Amazon?'

'There's no need to go to Amazon. Give me your business card and I'll make sure you get a copy.'

I gave him my business card.

A week later, his book landed on my desk.

The book was in English. Although Tsunenari had written the original in Japanese, mine was the English version, as translated by his son.

Over the weekend I read the book.

'How did you find it?' a friend asked, when I told him I had finished reading the book.

'I liked it. Two of his comments stay stuck in my mind,' I said.

'And what are they?' he said.

'He writes about the behaviour of Japanese people. He says they are disciplined, considerate of others and that they follow rules. And since they closely observe rules, they wrongly assume that everyone else does.'

'That I know – they are disciplined,' he said.

'He says that when Japanese people use pedestrian crossings, they start walking the exact instant the light turns green. They assume car drivers will stop. But the rest of the world may not have the same behavioural standards.'

'So?'

'Let me tell you how he puts it – he writes: "Whenever I am in China, my colleagues drum into me to be cautious crossing the streets – even if the pedestrian light is green. Japanese visitors who start crossing a busy intersection just as the 'walk' light is changing and at times also gazing into their mobile phone displays, run the risk of not living very long in China." I find it funny the way he phrased it.'

'And what was the other comment?'

'His book also addresses the Japanese idea of "kogi". This was the concept whereby every Japanese had a duty to do his or her part. All roles were thus clearly defined. The Emperor's was to reign with benevolence. The shogun's was to maintain peace and to protect the country.'

'And what about the samurais'?'

'That's just what I wanted to tell you about. Their role was to serve the shogun. By providing military service. His book explains that tradesmen and peasants had to be productive. Samurais, however, had no such responsibilities. And since they need not engage in labour, in return, they were to pursue "moral ways".'

'Meaning what, "moral ways"?' he said.

'They were not to tell jokes. Samurais were not to discuss business or lustful matters. They were not to get entangled with doing what they liked. Rather, they should be keen to do what they disliked.'

'That's interesting.'

'Tsunenari further comments in his book: "What we can deduce from all this moralising is that being a samurai was no fun at all."'…

69

Turkish Delights

Bodrum, Turkey

'Ladies and gentlemen, boys and girls.' This was how Chief Anyouku often started his speeches. Whenever he spoke, I and everyone else would listen attentively as his loud and booming voice immediately commanded our attention.

Emeka Anyouku is a Nigerian Chief. Educated in the United Kingdom, he is a tall man who holds himself upright, cutting an impressive figure. We all address him as "Chief". He had previously been a Nigerian foreign affairs minister and was for many years Secretary General of the Commonwealth of Nations.

We were in Bodrum, Turkey, attending an outdoor dinner. Our host was Akin Ongor, President of WWF Turkey. Akin was formerly a star basketball player with the Turkish national team. From sports he had moved on to banking and had risen to the position of CEO (Chief Executive Officer) of Garanti Bank, an important Turkish banking institution. That evening, we were gathered within the sprawling gardens of one of Akin's many homes.

Stepping up to a wooden podium, Chief addressed us.

'Ladies and gentlemen, boys and girls,' he said, in his hallmark low, resonating voice.

I looked around. There were neither boys nor girls in sight – we were all adults.

'Speeches are similar to ladies' skirts – not too long and therefore not interesting. But not too short – and yet long enough to cover the essentials.'

I laughed at his pun.

Chief continued, 'There was a village in Africa, where a pregnant woman was giving birth. There was no electricity, so to make it easier for the midwife, an illiterate neighbour was asked to hold a torch. As the midwife delivered the baby, the torch-holding neighbour became horrified. He had never assisted at a birth – and he had hardly recovered when another baby arrived. He started to tremble. A minute later, a third baby came on the scene. Then, as a fourth baby started on its way, the illiterate neighbour screamed.

"No!" he cried, as he ran out of the room.

"What are you doing? Come back here!" the midwife yelled.

"No! I must not. The light keeps attracting more of them," said the man.'

Following that introduction, Chief thanked our dinner host and the event sponsors. References were then made to WWF Turkey's conservation work with appropriate recognition and praise lavished upon deserving recipients. Special mention and recognition was made for Luc Hoffmann's long-standing commitment to the conservation cause.

Chief stepped off the podium.

Akin informed us that we would be treated to an astounding performance.

A man appeared on the stage. He had on a white shirt, a short white jacket and white pants. Over his trousers he wore a long white skirt. He was a Turkish swirling dancer. When he danced, it was by way of turning, swirling faster and ever faster. Due to his turning movements, his ample skirt gradually rose and eventually he looked like someone wearing an umbrella that hung from his hips and which hovered magically over his pants. His was a religious dance, a dance that was seven hundred years old. Never having seen such a performance before, I was fascinated.

When the dance was completed, it came time for dinner. The arrangements were such that we sat in several scattered groups, spread out over the many terraces of the sprawling house. It was a warm evening and I enjoyed the meal.

After dinner, we were asked to proceed to the swimming pool area.

'Surely not for a swim?' my chair-to-the-right-dinner-neighbour said.

'No, I don't think so,' I replied.

'I wonder why, then.'

We proceeded to the brightly lit poolside area. As I arrived, I bumped into Laurent Somé. He was with Doris, his wife. They were sitting on a low wall that was actually the cement circular enclosure of a large tree.

'Hey, come sit with us,' said Laurent.

I sat with them.

'You know what's happening next?' I asked.

'No,' he said.

'Ah, but I know,' said Doris. 'You chaps have found the right seating – just right, not too far away,' she added.

'What do you mean?' I said.

Before she could reply, I heard loud Turkish music. But nothing happened for a few seconds. And then I saw her. From behind some bushes, an attractive young woman appeared. She was a dancer – a different kind of dancer this time. In tune with the music, she entered the scene, gyrating her hips as she arrived. As she danced, the belly dancer headed towards the pool, passing right by in front of Laurent and myself on her way there.

'See, I told you chaps that you had found the right seating,' said Doris.

Arriving at the poolside, she initially performed alone. Then she decided she needed a stage prop. Without any interruption in how she moved her body (it must have been hundreds of vibrations per minute) she went straight to one of the WWF male colleagues. The colleague made not the slightest protest as she led him to a waiting chair. She sat him down. She continued to entertain all of us but especially the chosen colleague. She smiled at him. She twisted and she turned her body in front of him. She made her belly move like undulating waves. She shivered her shoulders left to right and she teased and taunted him in a hundred different ways. As she danced, she moved close to him. Very near but most artfully, she made sure that there was never any physical contact. Her teasing continued to the amusement of all of us.

Then she decided it was time to look for a new victim. Suddenly, she looked up, away from the entranced colleague on the chair. And she set her eyes on Chief. Without taking her eyes off him, she spread out both arms and she belly-danced in Chief's direction, making steady headway towards him. Chief, startled and realising what was happening or, rather, what might soon be happening to him, turned and started to run. She, seeing her victim trying to escape, stopped dancing. She ran after Chief and I was treated to a most unusual poolside scene. That of one scantily-clad belly dancer, literally chasing after a traditionally-dressed Nigerian Chief…

Farewell

70

Archbishop Tutu

Zurich, Switzerland

David Attenborough had just finished talking. Through multiple big screens scattered around the large hall, he had addressed us via video conferencing and had conveyed his support for the cause. After Attenborough had bade us goodbye and the screens went blank, the Master of Ceremonies resumed his role.

'There's someone else unable to attend tonight. He, too, he sends his warm greetings. The Duke of Edinburgh is not here with us this evening. But he asked me to tell you that it was impossible for him to attend tonight as he has a "family event" [the marriage of Kate and William].'

I laughed, as did everyone else.

'And now – I would like to introduce you to our very special keynote speaker. Someone you have all heard of. A person we all respect. Ladies and gentlemen, please welcome the Most Reverend Dr Desmond Tutu.'

Enthusiastic applause filled the entire room. I observed him intently as he walked towards the podium. Not tall and with a slight stoop, the Archbishop walked slowly, taking his time. Whilst small in size, there was no doubt as to his immense presence. There he was, the great man. He had spoken against apartheid. He had been awarded not only the Nobel Peace Prize but also the Albert Schweitzer Prize for Humanitarianism, not to mention the Gandhi Peace Prize. He had stood up for the oppressed. He had campaigned to fight not only Aids and tuberculosis but also homophobia and poverty and racism. And that evening, he was with us, as our important guest speaker.

I was one of the guests of Babar Ali for the evening – the Golden Jubilee 50th Anniversary celebrations of WWF. There were about six hundred people gathered in the event hall that evening, all observing

Desmond Tutu as he slowly walked towards the podium. Quietly, gently, he ascended the rostrum.

Approaching the microphone, the retired archbishop said, 'Ladies and gentlemen – do you know what you've done? You've given the microphone to a preacher. Now *this* is what I call a captive audience. The doors are now closed. You have no choice but to listen to me.

I come from South Africa – a beautiful country. We have two oceans. We have majestic high mountains and we have green forests. There is much wildlife. One can live a good life in my country.

And yet… amongst all this beauty there is the other side of the coin. We also have extreme poverty and there is intense suffering. There is inequality in the distribution of wealth. There is greed in the constant hunt for profit. More and evermore profit. Ah, profit, dollars and cents. And the problem is that this is the case, not only in my country, but also throughout the world.

When I look at what is happening on our planet – in our everlasting pursuit of profit – we are destroying the environment. And yet, at the same time, money is spent on armaments when only a small fraction of the amounts so used can do so much to help the poor. But this is how things are. Greed's a problem and, linked to that, damage to the environment. Harm to the Earth. This Earth. Our Earth. The *only* Earth we have. All this is indeed a very sad state of affairs. It really saddens me to see all this.'

Desmond Tutu looked up as he pointed to the ceiling.

'And you know – you know, above, there's our God. He sees all this. And He weeps. God cries. I tell you.

He really weeps – but all of a sudden, He stops crying.

God smiles – He smiles because down here, He sees WWF…'

END

Various appendices on the pages that follow provide supplementary information.

Appendix I

Summarized WWF History

In Switzerland, during the year 1961, a group of far-sighted men gathered in a private house. They met in Morges, a picturesque Swiss town located along the shores of Lake Geneva, and together they founded WWF – the World Wildlife Fund.

It so happened that at the same time as when these men convened, Chi-Chi the giant panda (at London Zoo) was increasingly popular and was often featured in the British media. Inspired by Chi-Chi, Gerald Watterson, the Scottish naturalist, sketched a few preliminary panda designs. Using one of these sketches as a model, Peter Scott subsequently created the panda logo.

Since its creation, WWF has grown and has systematically extended its reach. Today, it addresses not only wildlife but also wider conservation issues. Initially, WWF's activities were concentrated on the protection of wildlife. Subsequently, activities extended into other areas, as was planned from the beginning.

Incremental activities included protection of geographical areas where wildlife was located, as wildlife cannot be saved if their habitats are destroyed. Conservation work further expanded to include the needs of humans living in or near wildlife habitats, as well as covering wider issues such as climate change, which in turn influences habitat. Another area of activity where environmentalists can really make an impact on global subjects such as climate change is the influencing of laws and regulations. It is for this reason that WWF has currently not only field projects but also lobbying offices in cities where policy makers are located, such as Brussels and Washington. In today's modern world, influencing law makers has become as important a conservation activity as fieldwork and at times even more so where certain issues are concerned.

As the years passed, to better align its name to activities that now encompassed much more than wildlife and to communicate this extended reach to the world, WWF – the then World Wildlife Fund – changed its name to WWF, the Worldwide Fund for Nature. Thus the word "Wildlife" that was to be found in its previous name was dropped, whilst the initials "WWF" remained unchanged.

WWF is today a well-known and highly respected global conservation organisation. With a presence in more than a hundred countries, it has close to five million supporters and annual revenues approaching a billion US dollars. Its funding initially came primarily from individuals. Today, however, income originates not only from individuals, who, as a group, continue to constitute an important income source, but also from corporations, foundations and from governments. In addition, WWF has its own revenue stream, consisting of financial income arising from investments, as well as royalties. In general, funds raised in developed countries are spent in emerging countries.

Appendix II

Different WWF Names

As mentioned in Appendix I, WWF was initially called World Wildlife Fund. Later, it changed its name to Worldwide Fund for Nature. However, in the US and in Canada, it continues to be known as the World Wildlife Fund. In Switzerland there are two legal entities bearing the initials WWF in their name. Firstly, there is WWF Switzerland, a national organisation (national organisations being WWF legal entities set up in different countries, with their own board of trustees) with headquarters in Zurich. There is also the "original", this being the WWF International Secretariat.

The International Secretariat is located in Gland, near Geneva. It is commonly referred to as "WWF International" although this is a non-existent legal name. The official legal name of WWF International is rather long and cumbersome and quite a mouthful to pronounce.

The official name of the WWF Secretariat, as used on all legal documents, is as follows:

"WWF Worldwide Fund for Nature (formerly the World Wildlife Fund)."

The most common use of the organisation's name is in the form of the three initials, "WWF". However, this can at times give rise to confusion. Often, these initials are confused with the WWF of the World Wrestling Federation/Entertainment. I have myself experienced much such confusion. Two examples follow:

'Oh, so you work for WWF! My ten-year-old son – he just loves watching your programmes. He's a great wrestling fan,' said the man sitting next to me on the plane.

'I see, WWF,' said the UK customs official when I arrived at Heathrow Airport. 'Which one: the wrestlers or the environmental group?' he asked.

'Do I look like a wrestler?' I replied and he laughed.

But of all the harmless mix-ups I have encountered, the one I like best is when I received office mail addressed to "WWF, World Wine Federation".

Julian Huxley

Julian Huxley, a British biologist, was the first Director General of UNESCO – the United Nations Educational, Scientific and Cultural Organisation. Before he founded WWF, Julian had already played an important role in the founding of another influential conservation organisation. This was the IUCN – the International Union for the Conservation of Nature.

When Huxley first visited East Africa in the 1930s, he went with the intention of encouraging the creation of national parks. He made a return trip in 1960 with the intention of briefing UNESCO concerning the state of nature conservation in East Africa. During his second trip, what he witnessed alarmed him. The teeming wildlife he had previously seen no longer existed. In addition, he found that the intensive hunting of the larger fauna was seriously threatening certain species with extinction.

Upon his return to Great Britain, Huxley decided to alert public opinion whereupon he wrote numerous articles in *The Observer* newspaper. Many readers responded, including Victor Stolan, a businessman. Stolan advised Huxley to found an international organisation – not any organisation but one influential enough to raise sufficient funds to effectively contribute towards the combat for the preservation of bio-diversity. To ensure that the organisation so created would be effective, Stolan further recommended that Huxley contact eminent scientists to co-found the organisation and thus was sown the seeds for the founding of WWF.

Original Founders

The six founders of WWF were Julian Huxley, Max Nicholson, Peter Scott, Hans Hussy, Luc Hoffmann and Guy Montfort. The first two vice-presidents were Peter Scott and Luc Hoffmann.

Max Nicholson was an ornithologist and the then Director General of Britain's Nature Conservancy. Peter Scott was an ornithologist. Hans Hussy is a Swiss lawyer whilst Luc Hoffmann is an ornithologist. Guy Montfort was an ornithologist too.

Peter Scott

The ornithologist Peter Scott was a man of many talents. In addition to being an Olympic yachtsman, he was a much-liked television presenter, a gliding champion, a painter, a naturalist and last but certainly not least, a skipper in the America's Cup.

Preserving the Antarctic was one of his driving interests. His father was none other than Robert Falcon Scott, popularly known as "Scott of the Antarctic", who died there when Peter Scott was not yet two years old. Knighted in 1973, Peter Scott was the first conservationist to receive a knighthood.

Supplementary Information

PART ONE – Goodbye Corporations

1 – Do Fire Me

Digital Equipment Corporation (DEC) was well reputed for its mini-computers. The company's "PDP" and "VAX" products had excellent reputations and were much in demand – they sold like "hot cakes". DEC was subsequently taken over by Compaq in 1998 and Compaq, in turn, was bought by Hewlett Packard. That was in 2002. When I left DEC in 1991, the total headcount of Europe-based employees engaged in the finance function exceeded a thousand people.

2 – At Home

Home in those days was in a quiet residential region near Geneva called Tannay, situated in the canton of Vaud, some fifteen minutes' drive from Geneva town centre.

PART TWO – Landing on Planet WWF

4 – Passing Jaguar

The offices of WWF International, the international secretariat in Switzerland, are located approximately thirty minutes' drive from Geneva town and about the same in terms of driving time from Geneva Airport. It's in a town called Gland. Whilst WWF staff often mention to outsiders, "We're in Geneva", in reality the offices are located not in the state of Geneva, but in the neighbouring state of Vaud.

Whenever I drive my car along Lake Geneva from Geneva to Lausanne I pass small towns and picturesque villages and at times the scenery can be stunning. Along certain stretches on a clear day I can see the blue waters of Lake Geneva and the mountains in France on the far side of the lake. On sunny summer days the white sails of numerous sailboats dotting the lake can be visible.

I sometimes joked with foreign visitors, "If you want to find us, that's easy. Hire a car and take the scenic route from Geneva to Lausanne. Drive leisurely and enjoy the view. You'll see picturesque towns; but at a certain stage of your drive you will suddenly find yourself in an unprepossessing area. When that occurs, stop. You have found Gland – that's where the WWF offices are."

The WWF building in Gland has an interesting history.

Some years in the past, the chairman of the then Swiss Bank Corporation (SBC) was a trustee of WWF. The SBC (which has since merged with UBS) was then one of the three large Swiss banks, which consisted of Credit Suisse, SBC and UBS (Union Bank of Switzerland). At that time, when WWF was looking for office space, it so happened that one of the clients of the SBC had financial difficulties and was looking to sell their building. Due to the initiative of the SBC-linked WWF International Board Trustee, a donor was identified, enabling the purchase of the building. That was how WWF came to own the first (in later years I had subsequently negotiated with Philips Electronics for the acquisition of a second building) building in Gland. Although it's an unattractive structure, in terms of functionality it does the job. Functional it is and not luxurious, which is perfect, given the nature of the organisation's activity. Would you rush to donate money to a not-for-profit organisation housed in luxury premises?

The bank's client that had owned the building was a manufacturer of money-counting machines. To test their machines, they had to keep stacks of money. Real cash was needed, in order to have the right texture and sizes of the different bank notes for machine testing. At the end of each day, the banknotes so employed were re-deposited back in the basement – in vaults and thus securely kept behind huge safe doors. The hefty vault doors are six foot high and six inches thick, extremely heavy and expensive to remove. They still stand there today, in the basement, keeping solemn guard over unimportant and mostly forgotten files. I had at times offered these imposing doors to visiting bankers for free. Each time I received instant smiles in return. Likely it's because I had always specified one non-negotiable condition. I would tell the bankers, yes, the doors are free, but they're on a self-service basis…

6 – Job Interview

The early model electric car belonged to Peter Kramer, who was then the Director of Conservation. A few months after I was hired, Peter took me for a spin in his car. The experience was not as uncomfortable as I had initially imagined, but then we only went for a short drive.

PART FOUR – Environmental Conservation

15 – Rebellious Youngsters

I was most fascinated by a documentary I once saw. It was shot by the Cousteau Foundation and was about spiny lobsters travelling in line. They do this once each year, the lobsters, travelling between eight to ten kilometres every twenty-four hours. The entire journey covers around 100 kilometres. The travelling method they use is fascinating because each lobster, using its pincers, "holds" the lobster directly in front, thus forming a long "lobster-train".

18 – Game Wardens Shoot Poachers

Firing rifles into the air is likely to be no longer the case today. In some countries poachers and wardens do have dangerous real shoot-outs.

19 – Locked Safe

Was the safe recovered? Yes, police subsequently found the safe. It had been abandoned in the forest. The door was open and the cash was gone. However, no financial loss was suffered as the insurers subsequently reimbursed WWF.

21 – Room Service

Mauritania's local currency is the Ouguiya, the Mauritanian rupee, which is divisible into one hundred smaller units, the UM. The rate for my green room was 10,000 UM, equivalent to 100 Ouguiya. At an exchange rate of approximately 0.03 USD to one Ouguiya, my room cost was 30 USD. No wonder the facilities were somewhat limited. Camel stew, if I had ordered it, was, in relative terms, expensive. If I had ordered it, it would have set me back 15 USD, half my room rate.

25 – Entry Formalities

In this particular case of dishonesty, over a hundred thousand US dollars had beenmisappropriated by one of the WWF country managers. The manager had written WWF cheques for her personal expenditures and the bank had made the payments. However, the bank should not have paid as the cheques had only one signature – whereas the bank signature authorisation card stated that two signatures were mandatory for cheque payments. The local WWF country office had asked the bank to repay the sums so lost but the bank had flatly refused to do so. Their argument was that they had acted in good faith. Their reasoning was that, after all, it was not a junior employee but the WWF country manager herself who had written the fraudulent cheques and they had no reason to doubt the validity of the payments. The WWF lawyers in the project country and the bank's lawyers had met. However, they could not agree upon any settlement terms.

It was under such circumstances that I said to Laurent that I would visit the country and would give it a shot. I would try to recover our losses, at least a part of them, or, ideally, all of them. When I arrived in the country, together with Laurent, we called upon the local law firm appointed by WWF for the matter. When I was there at the lawyer's offices, the lawyer showed us a harsh letter from the bank's lawyers that mentioned that the bank disowned any liability whatsoever and would not be willing to repay anything. Our lawyer commented that it was quite certain we would not recoup a single dollar. Whilst I understood our lawyer, I did not agree with his conclusions. I therefore asked Laurent to arrange a meeting with the bank manager, stating I did not wish any lawyers to be present at the meeting, neither ours, nor the bank's.

A meeting was scheduled. Laurent and I set off to meet with the bank manager. The bank was South African owned and the manager was French. When we met, he was friendly but firm in stating that they would not pay. In the meantime, however, I had written not only to the local country head office of the bank but also to the South African head office, setting out WWF's reasons for claiming repayment. When I met with the banker, together with Laurent, I made it clear to him, saying it in as polite a manner as possible, but at the same time leaving no doubt that I would do it, that I would kick up a real "stink" if his bank did not repay WWF. I assured him I would contact the media and relate how a big bank, through incompetence, had lost a substantial amount of monies of a not-for-profit organisation. After heated discussions, the bank manager eventually conceded. He agreed to the bank's liability. The bank would repay the entire amount: approximately 120,000 US dollars. I was to send a driver round the next day to collect the cheque. The following day an employee was sent to pick up the cheque – and that indeed proceeded smoothly. The cheque was banked and WWF's losses were entirely recouped.

29 – Have Cash Will Travel

Apart from the Georgia case, where the amounts of funds carried were relatively unimportant, there was one temporary period when I had authorised substantial sums to be carried in cash. This was for Russia, in 1998, when the banking system there did not work efficiently and I could not find any bank in Switzerland willing to wire transfer sums there, except at our own risk that the monies would arrive. And yet, projects there had to be financed so that conservation work could continue uninterrupted. During that short period, I mandated a company that specialised in transporting money, Brinks, to transport the cash.

34 – Dive Bomber

There are around 30,000 crows in Tokyo. Some of them do attack people, especially people riding bicycles. It's been reported cyclists have fallen off their bikes when chased by crows. The birds are not afraid of humans and should someone try to scare them off, they become even more aggressive. Local officials are trying to lower their population by removing eggs from their nests.

35 – Malaysian Way

In addition to the Leatherback, other examples of turtle species are: Green Turtle, Hawksbill, Olive Ridley and Painted Terrapins.

It was close to midnight when we went down to the beach to release the baby turtles. Intuitively, each one of them, using their fins, they paddled towards the sea, joining the gently lapping waves. Perhaps it was the slope of the beach, or the sound of the waves, or both, or it might be due to other factors, but they all knew exactly which direction to take. Pushing with their fins, in a left to right swaying movement, each turtle made its way towards the sea. And wherever they passed, they left tiny traces of baby turtle walking marks on the sand.

Sea turtles have a long life span but most of them die young, eaten up by fishes and other natural predators. The few who survive live for many years. Marine turtles are an ancient species. They are as old as the dinosaurs and that means a hundred million years old. Living most of their lives at sea, turtles are mobile, graceful and well adapted to their environment. Amazing animals, they can even slow their heartbeat down to only one pulse every nine minutes.

Today, the survival of this remarkable animal is threatened by many different factors, including pollution, changes to their habitat, being accidentally drowned when caught in fishing nets, or because their eggs are eaten not only by humans but also by foxes, pigs and dogs. The list of threats to them is long.

Although turtles spend most of their lives at sea, they return to land to lay their eggs. By some system yet unknown, they find their way back to where they were born. That night, when we released the baby turtles, I was on a secluded beach. Apart from the sound of waves lapping softly on the sand, the place was quiet. There were coconut trees along the shores and the whole scene was extremely peaceful. And yet I knew that, not too far away, about five kilometres away, buildings could be found. And not only that, there was even an oil refinery complex.

Each released hatchling soon reached the sea. The waves splashed on their backs and they disappeared, swallowed up by the immense South China Sea. Most of them will not survive. A miniscule minority will make it, one in ten thousand. Some thirty to forty years later, some of these survivors, the females, will return. But, by then, what will they find when they come back? Will it be the same sandy, secluded beach? Or will they find a hotel, complete with sun decks, umbrellas, swimming pools, tourists, ice-cream vendors and music? As a species they have been around for over one hundred million years. And yet, when some of these ancient creatures return, in "only" forty years' time, what indeed will they find?

36 – Repeat Three Initials

The Living Planet Fund was launched in 2003. André Hoffmann and I were the joint founders. I first discussed the concept of a WWF-sponsored investment fund with André in 1999 when we were both in Borneo, attending a WWF annual conference. We had the goal of developing it into an important investment fund, whereby a percentage of the management fees would be used to finance environmental projects. Environmental projects in general and the funding of less attractive items in particular – for example, funding to pay for necessary functions such as internal audits. After our discussions, it took us a few years to convince all the relevant WWF colleagues, after which we had to convince the WWF International Executive Committee as well as the Board of Trustees. Then, the investment strategy had to be outlined and had to be agreed upon by all relevant colleagues, including obtaining the agreement of the more important National Organisations. But that was not all that we had to do. Following that, we had to obtain approvals from the various regulatory authorities. This included the authorities in Luxembourg representing the European Union, as well as the authorities in the main countries where the fund was to be marketed, these being Germany, Switzerland, France and the United Kingdom.

The fund was then launched in 2003. At the same time I had established a Luxembourg incorporated management company, called the Living Planet Fund Management Company, to manage the fund. This corporation was structured as a subsidiary of WWF International and I obtained the funds needed for its share capital from a donor.

However, some years after the fund's creation, WWF (in 2012) had a change of strategy and wished to exit the investment fund business. The management of the fund was transferred in 2013 to FundPartners Solutions, a Pictet company (private bankers headquartered in Geneva). FundPartners Solutions became the new managers and they in turn have delegated, via a mandate, to Coninco (a company based in Vevey, Switzerland, founded by Olivier Ferrari, who is the Chief Executive Officer) the management of the portfolio. Coninco was given the mandate for the sake of continuity – they had been the managers delegated by the Living Planet Fund Management Company.

When I co-founded the fund in 2003 the fund size was five million US dollars. When it was transferred in 2013, the fund exceeded fifty million US dollars. In 2014, it exceeded seventy million euros, which is approximately 100 million USD. As part of the transfer to Pictet arrangements, the fund had a name change and was renamed "One Sustainable Fund".

37 – Hand in the Honey Pot

Most bees produce honey. Honeybees refer to bees that produce honey in sufficient quantities to make harvesting by man worthwhile. There are the common domesticated honeybees and there are those found in the wild. Altogether there are less than twenty species (between seven and eleven depending on whom you talk to) of honeybees and some forty subspecies. Compared with bees in general, honeybees are relatively rare. This is because whilst there are less than twenty species of honeybees, there exists twenty thousand known species of bees.

PART FIVE – Royalty

39 – Lost In Buckingham Palace

The handful of times I had lunch at the palace, I found it a treat. We would typically be a small group, between six to eight people sitting around a large, dark, wooden oval table. Prince Philip would sit in the middle and we would take seats around the rest of the table.

I recall having in front of me, as did everyone else, a small printed menu. In addition, there was no need to ask anyone to pass the salt and pepper. We each had a salt and pepper set in front of us. The tableware was of the highest quality. All the crystal glasses had two letters, "ER", standing for "Elizabeth Regina'" distinctly engraved on them and facing us. I would have liked to have had taken home with me one of each of the table items as a souvenir but of course did not take any. I did once take home a printed menu. However, a few days later, not knowing what to do with it, I threw it away.

We were always served British mineral water, either still or sparkling and for the main meal the accompanying wine would be an excellent glass of full-bodied dark red French claret. The meals were always tasty, well presented and balanced. Each meal was timed so that it did not linger on.

Some Interesting Buckingham Palace Facts And Figures:

Facts and figures about Buckingham Palace, as per information I extracted from the official website of the British Monarchy (www.royal.gov.uk).

- The palace has 775 rooms.
- The total floor area is 77,000 square metres; no wonder I got lost.
- The palace site was originally a mulberry garden to rear silkworms.
- There are 1,514 doors; unauthorised, I only opened one.
- Some rooms have a Chinese theme.
- Home to thirty bird species and 350 different wild flowers.
- Suffered nine direct bomb hits during the Second World War.
- There are 350 clocks and watches.
- There are two full-time clock conservators.
- Visitors include Mozart when he was all of seven years old.
- Another was Mahatma Gandhi, who wore a loincloth and sandals to drink tea with King George V.

42 – Playing Truant

Of the different WWF country board presidents I have met, one of the persons I especially appreciate is Syed Babar Ali, of WWF Pakistan. Babar's President Emeritus of WWF Pakistan. He's also Vice-President Emeritus of WWF International, an elite club comprising of only two persons – him and Luc Hoffmann. The President Emeritus is HRH Prince Philip.

In terms of his relationship with WWF, Babar had been at different times, President of WWF Pakistan, Treasurer of WWF International and President of WWF International. Babar is a charming gentleman. He is elegant, courteous and good company to be with. I always enjoyed his company.

Often we used to have dinner together when he visited Geneva or London. In addition to dinner, we would take walks together – sometimes before a meal and at other times after a meal. We have taken walks in London and in Geneva; in the Swiss countryside region of Mies where I live; in Gland near Geneva where the WWF offices are located; in Vienna near the Opera House; in Tanjong Aru in Borneo; in Berlin; in Lausanne and in Montreux in Switzerland; in Lahore in Pakistan and in Karachi, to name but a few examples. When we walk together, it's always at a steady pace. Not a stroll and yet not a run. A pace quick enough to make the walk interesting but not too fast that we cannot appreciate whatever sights and sounds we encounter – and certainly not so fast that we become breathless and therefore unable to converse.

43 – Royal President's Remarks

During my watch as Finance Director and especially during my early years with WWF, HRH Prince Philip was very active in his role as President of WWF International. It is for this reason that this book has a section that refers to royalty. It is also thanks to Prince Philip that we had increased access to personalities and organisations for conservation purposes, not to mention the funds we were able to raise because of his involvement. Amongst ourselves, we used to refer to Prince Philip as "HRH". When we were talking with him, we used to address him as 'sir' as he did not like to be addressed along the lines of "Your Royal Highness".

Prince Philip always signed documents as "Philip". It was because of how he signed that I learnt important persons did just that – sign documents using only their forenames, rather than their full names.

44 – Prince Albert's Authorisation

Prince Albert refers to Prince Albert II of Monaco. His official title is HSH – His Serene Highness. The Prince has a keen interest in conservation and in WWF. His conservation activities include the creation of a foundation for conservation matters, the Foundation Prince Albert II of Monaco, based in Monaco.

Apart from the Panda Ball held in Monaco, Prince Albert also attended other WWF functions, including a Panda Ball held in Montreux, Switzerland. During that function, I was most impressed with his patience when I saw the stream of women coming to him to ask for a photograph to be taken with him – and how he patiently obliged each time.

45 – Only Sara Dares

Cota Donana is an estuary south of Seville. Not only is it home to the world's most endangered cat, the Iberian Lynx, it's also a stopping point for six million birds, including thousands of flamingoes. Protection of the Cota Donana was one of WWF's first great conservation efforts.

Luc Hoffmann was instrumental in securing protection for Cota Donana in the 1960s. Luc is not only one of the founders of WWF but over the years has been one of its greatest supporters. Since then andré Hoffmann, his son, has also joined the ranks of being a major contributor to the WWF cause.

The Hon. Sara Morrison, FRSA, has had a wide-ranging and extensive career covering not only business but also public service. In addition to having acted as President of WWF International, she was at one time Chairperson of WWF UK. Sara has long-standing involvements with community and voluntary organisations in Wiltshire, where she lives and runs a farm. In all my dealings with her, I have always found Sara extremely bright, cheerful and a pleasure to be with. She would make excellent and relevant remarks at meetings and she would quickly bring down to size any person behaving badly at meetings.

46 – Danish Way

The Danish monarchy is one of the oldest in the world – about a thousand years old. His Royal Highness, Henrik, the Prince Consort, born Henri Jean André Count Laborde de Monpezat, is one of WWF's supporters. Johan Schroeder is also the Honorary Consul-General for New Zealand in Denmark

47 – Rascal

It's very British to make understatements or to say the exact opposite as a sign of affection.

48 – Her Serene Highness

Tatiana told me her lineage dates from 1400 and was therefore older than the Romanovs. The Romanovs date from 1613, until the overthrow of the monarchy in 1917.

49 – King Of Tonga

I, too, used to think, wrongly, that the country of Tonga was located in Africa. Wikipedia states: "The country is located in the South Pacific Ocean and is made up of close to two hundred islands, of which only fifty are inhabited. The only monarchy in the Pacific Ocean, it is sometimes referred to as "The Friendly Islands", a name that has its origin in the friendly reception given to Captain James Cook during his first visit to the islands in 1773."

51 – What One Greek Said

Jain priests wear a cloth scarf over their noses and mouths so as to ensure they do not, by mistake, breathe in any insects. This practice is linked to the core concept of Jainism, non-violence, which encompasses compassion and universal love for all living creatures.

Prince Philip was born Prince of Greece and Denmark, at the Greek Royal residence of Mon Repos on the island of Corfu in 1921. Prince Andrew, younger brother of King Constantine of Greece, and Princess Alice of Battenburg were his parents.

PART SIX – Fundraising

52 – Let's Get Them

Sometimes legacies can arrive quite easily. At one time I received news from one of my finance department staff members that one of the Nordic offices had received a large legacy that exceeded a million US dollars. To find out more, I called the finance manager of that WWF country office. Often I'm interested, not only in the results, but also as to how things happened – the origin, finding out what was the trigger or the driver for events that occurred.

'How did that legacy arise?' I asked.

I was told that an elderly lady went to see her local bank manager. She wanted to bequest a sum to a worthwhile cause but was uncertain which to pick. Her banker had replied, 'How about WWF?'

And that was it, how the legacy came about, as simple as that.

53 – St James's Palace Dinner

St James's Palace was built during the 16th century. It was constructed by Henry Tudor; the King who had six wives: two he divorced, one died, two he executed and, finally, one he left a widow. St James's Palace is so called because it was built on the site of the Hospital of St James in Westminster.

It was in St James's Palace that Mary Tudor, the only surviving child from Henry Tudor's first wife, signed the treaty that surrendered Calais to the French and it was there she died. It was also there where Elizabeth I resided when the Spanish Armada was threatening Britain.

54 – Insider's View

Did she manage to get her grandchildren there? Yes, she did. Since her family were (at that time) important donors, a colleague rang the palace and that was arranged.

56 – His Big Toe

Bank Sarasin was merged in 2013 with Bank Safra. The new entity is called Bank J. Safra Sarasin.

It's probably appropriate that the Cercle de la Terrasse, being much frequented by bankers, is located on Rue Jean-Gabriel Eynard. A banker, Eynard lived 1777-1863. The foundation of his immense fortune came about because he was the sole subscriber to a bond offering issued by the Duke of Etruria (Tuscany, Italy).

One document that crossed my desk was literally written on the back of an envelope. It was a pledge signed by the late Robert Maxwell shortly before his death at sea. Did WWF collect on this pledge? I did contact the liquidators/receivers – but no, there was no collection possible.

59 – Pecking Order

On the listed table, "Duke" is just before "King" and therefore has a higher ranking than "Prince" – this is per the European table. In the United Kingdom, the title "Prince" is more important.

PART SEVEN – Business Unusual

60 – City Bankers

What happened to the bankers? After the bankers had vacated the room, the Investment Committee held its formal meeting. As agenda item number one, we discussed whether the bankers would be retained. It took less than one second for the committee to unanimously agree upon the termination of the bankers' mandate.

63 – His Ego Trip

During another flight, I heard a different kind of flight announcement. As my Air France flight approached our destination's airport, a low male voice spoke over the speaker-system: 'Ladies and gentlemen, please fasten your seat belts. It's because we have begun our descent. That's probably a good idea – no point in staying indefinitely in the air…'

In Yaoundé, Cameroon, on a small dusty landing strip, I approached the single-propeller plane. I saw the pilot making the sign of the cross.

'In the name of the Father and of the Son and of the Holy Ghost…'

Iain Carr, a WWF colleague saw the look on my face. 'Don't worry. This is a missionary plane – all their pilots do that,' he said.

64 – Swiss Watches

Bilan, a Swiss business magazine, per issue dated 27ᵗʰ April 2011, informed me as follows:

"Ulysse Nardin, the Swiss watchmakers, was founded in 1846. When the firm encountered difficulties and was down to one sole watchmaker, Rolf Schnyder bought it in 1983. Rolf systematically grew the company and, in 2011, the year he passed away aged seventy-five, the company employed some five hundred people with three hundred located in the region between Le Locle and La Chaux de Fonds in Switzerland."

Watches remind me of time slots:

'I must have that telephone conference,' I said to my assistant.

And so she arranged for the different participants to call in.

Since I was the person requesting the telephone conference and because the participants resided in four different continents, we had to set up a time so that the greatest inconvenience fell upon myself. With the timing skilfully co-ordinated by my secretary, the different participants were to call in, taking into account the varying time zones, as follows:

San Francisco, USA, a participant:	Monday 0800hrs
Paris, France, a participant:	Monday 1700hrs
Geneva, Switzerland, a participant:	Monday 1700hrs
Antananarivo, Madagascar, a participant:	Monday 1900hrs
Singapore, myself:	Tuesday 0000 hrs

And so the conference started with me having the midnight slot, whereupon I said to the participants, 'Thank you, everyone, for making time available. I have to tell you – for me, this conference, it's a double first. It's the first time I have joined a telephone conference at midnight. It's also the first time I'm participating in a conference whilst in my pyjamas.'

67 – Elephant God

We were being driven in a car called the Hindustan Ambassador. Many cars in India are Ambassadors. It's a quaint-looking vehicle based on the Morris Oxford, which was manufactured in the UK in the '50s. In production since the late '50s, without much modification, it's fondly called the "King of Indian roads".

68 – Samurai Warriors' Lot

When I met him, Tsunenari Tokugawa was the President of WWF Japan. A banker, he is the eighteenth head of the Tokugawa shogunai household that had been instituted by Tokugawa Leyasu in 1603. When the shogunate was established, Edo, the ancient name of Tokyo, was established as the seat of government. And that effectively made it the country's capital. The Emperor's residence remained in Kyoto, which had been the capital up to that time. The shogunate lasted until just before the Meiji Restoration in 1867.

69 – Turkish Delights

As he moved, the whirling dervish had the palm of his right hand facing the heavens whilst that of his left hand faced the earth. He turned because everything in the universe moves and turns, be it the solar system or the blood in our veins.

Appendix VII

Credits

Edo Inheritance	Tsunenari Tokugawa's book for the comments about samurai.
royal.gov.uk	The website consulted for information about Buckingham Palace.
Wikipedia	For various information.
WWF	Via the panda.org website for information about WWF.

Acknowledgements

I wish to express my special gratitude to the following people:

Bob Bishop, for writing the foreword of this book.
Hugh Wheelan, for the book's title.
Lin Cook, for the multiple proofreads.

In addition, I thank the following people for the high quality of professional services received:

Aimee Bell of Author Design Studio, for the book's website.
Gary Smailes of Bubblecow, for the editing.
Ed Grace, for the illustrations.
Ned Hoste of 2h Design, for the book's cover.
Jeremy Thompson & the Matador team, for various publication services.

Comments concerning not-for-profit organisations

211

'No one is useless in this world who lightens the burden of another.'

Charles Dickens (1812-1870)

In the spirit of Dickens' comment, whilst no contractual obligation requires it, a part of the royalties arising from the sales of this book will be given to certain not-for-profit organisations. Some of these entities will have an environmental mission, whilst others will have a humanitarian or other social purpose.

Chiew Y. Chong was born in Malaysia of Chinese parentage. Upon completion of his schooling at a Jesuit-run school in Kuala Lumpur, he set off for London. Qualifying as a chartered accountant, Chiew worked in the Far East and in Europe, where he held senior financial positions at a number of major international corporations.

In 1991, he decided he needed a change and, almost by accident, he joined WWF – Worldwide Fund for Nature. Chiew initially intended to stay for a year – at maximum, two. As it turned out, he found the work so engrossing and challenging he remained for several years with the organisation, leaving only in 2012.

At WWF, Chiew lived through a myriad of interesting and unforgettable events – being attacked by a mad crow was one. He met numerous exceptional, committed environmentalists, including HRH Prince Philip of the United Kingdom. After having spent two decades at WWF, Chiew decided he would write a book – to share at first hand his experiences, as seen through the eyes of someone coming from the corporate sector.

Contact information:
Email: cychong1000@gmail.com
Website: www.lifeonplanetwwf.com
Website: www.cychong-author.com
Twitter: @c_y_chong
Facebook: Life on Planet WWF